KETO

Sweet Tooth

COOKBOOK

KETO

Sweet Tooth

COOKBOOK

80 low-carb ketogenic dessert recipes
for cakes, cookies, pies, fat bombs,
shakes, ice cream, and more

AARON DAY
of *FatForWeightLoss*

ALPHA

Publisher Mike Sanders
Senior Editor Brook Farling
Senior Designer Jessica Lee
Art Director William Thomas
Photographer Kelley Schuyler
Food Stylist Savannah Norris
Proofreader Rick Kughen
Indexer Celia McCoy

First American Edition, 2019
Published in the United States by DK Publishing
6081 E. 82nd Street, Indianapolis, Indiana 46250

Copyright © 2019 Dorling Kindersley Limited
DK, a Division of Penguin Random House LLC
20 21 22 23 10 9 8 7 6 5 4
004–313892–July/2019

Published in the United States by Dorling Kindersley Limited

Note: This publication contains the opinions and ideas of its author(s). It is intended to provide helpful and informative material on the subject matter covered. It is sold with the understanding that the author(s) and publisher are not engaged in rendering professional services in the book. If the reader requires personal assistance or advice, a competent professional should be consulted. The author(s) and publisher specifically disclaim any responsibility for any liability, loss, or risk, personal or otherwise, which is incurred as a consequence, directly or indirectly, of the use and application of any of the contents of this book.

Trademarks: All terms mentioned in this book that are known to be or are suspected of being trademarks or service marks have been appropriately capitalized. Alpha Books, DK, and Penguin Random House LLC cannot attest to the accuracy of this information. Use of a term in this book should not be regarded as affecting the validity of any trademark or service mark.

A catalog record for this book is available from the Library of Congress.
ISBN 978-1-4654-8383-6
Library of Congress Catalog Number: 2019936905

DK books are available at special discounts when purchased in bulk for sales promotions, premiums, fund-raising, or educational use. For details, contact SpecialSales@dk.com

Printed and bound in China

A WORLD OF IDEAS:
SEE ALL THERE IS TO KNOW

www.dk.com

ABOUT THE AUTHOR

Aaron Day is an accredited nutritional therapist, clinical weight loss practitioner, and advanced sports exercise nutritional advisor. As an advocate for the ketogenic diet and keto lifestyle, he's the recipe developer, food photographer, and videographer behind the popular blog fatforweightloss.com.au, where he creates and shares delicious ketogenic recipes that are comforting, quick, and simple to make.

From living out his dream to cycle through Europe with nothing but a tent in tow, to climbing 4,500 meters in one-day cycling events, and to running marathons using the unusual endurance diet of high-fat, low-carb foods, Aaron is dedicated to pushing past what is deemed possible, and helping others to do the same. Through ambitious goals, Aaron has realized that it is not the outcome that you learn the most from, it's the journey and struggles along the way that make you better.

Contents

Welcome, fellow sweet tooths!

When I was younger, I grew up in an environment where I was surrounded by a wealth of health knowledge. There was an emphasis on consuming micronutrients, natural supplements, and an abundance of healthy foods, while avoiding foods that could produce allergies. But as I grew up and became a musician, I began to live a very frugal lifestyle that had a negative impact on my health and my endocrine system. I was overworked, tired, and underpaid; it was a recipe for malnourishment and subsequent digestive issues that were a direct result of my own poor food choices. To fix the problem, I began to study and research nutrition and discovered that fat was not the enemy, but rather, instead, carbohydrates and sugar were the enemies. I realized that if I could starve my body of the carbs and sugar it was using for fuel, my body would then turn to burning by own fat to create the energy it needed.

The "Fat For Weight Loss" name for my blog is a bit of a poke at what much of society thinks is making us all obese: fat. What we're learning is that, in fact, consuming fat while greatly reducing your carbohydrate intake can actually make you thin! That's where the ketogenic diet comes in. The ketogenic diet is a revolutionary way to lose weight and improve your health by changing how and what you eat. But, there's a catch. If you already follow the keto diet, you know you simply can't eat the sugar and carbs that are present in traditional sweets, and that means enjoying sweet treats is one of the biggest challenges about following the ketogenic diet. But what if you could create mouthwatering cookies, decadent cakes, luscious ice creams, and comforting pies that not only are healthy but will also help you stay in a fat burning mode? By purchasing this book, you've taken a big step toward doing just that.

The recipes in this book contain desserts that are not only keto-friendly; they're delicious and will satisfy anyone with a sweet tooth—even those sweet tooths who aren't doing keto! Best of all, they'll help you achieve your health goals without the sugar and carbs, which means you'll be following a lifestyle that will impart lasting changes to your health.

Following keto isn't always easy, and adopting a healthy lifestyle can be time consuming, costly, and require a lot of hard work, but going keto and utilizing your own biochemistry to change your health for the better is one of the most important and lasting changes you can make in your life. And the good news is that you can do it all without giving up dessert!

– Aaron Day

CHAPTER 1

Getting Started

This chapter will explain some of the essential ingredients, handy techniques, and useful equipment you'll be using to make your keto desserts and treats.

Making Keto Sweet

An essential part of following the ketogenic diet is eliminating most of the sugar and carbs from your diet. So where does that leave dessert? Is it really possible to enjoy sweet treats on a keto diet? Absolutely!

HOW KETO WORKS

If you've picked up this book, it's likely you already know that the ketogenic diet is a low-carb, high-fat diet that requires reducing carbohydrate intake to the point that your body begins burning stored fat for fuel. It's pretty simple: When you reduce carbohydrate intake to a point where your body can no longer rely on carbs as a primary source of energy, it flips a switch and begins accessing the fat stored in your body for energy. This process helps keep insulin levels low and also helps facilitate ketosis, which is the state in which your body—being starved for glucose—begins burning stored fat for fuel. This process also produces molecules in the liver called *ketones*, which are the by-products of the body breaking down these fatty acids.

HOW KETO DESSERTS ARE DIFFERENT

Most traditional sweets use ingredients like common sugar and wheat flour as primary ingredients. Keto desserts, however, can't contain these ingredients because of the high volume of carbs they contain. This means keto-friendly desserts need to be created a little differently in order to be low carb and sugar free. Keto desserts utilize sweeteners that are sugar free and have a low glycemic index, so words like *erythritol* and *stevia* will soon become a part of your kitchen vocabulary. Additionally, keto desserts can't contain wheat flour, and instead, they are made with lower-carb nut flours like almond flour and coconut flour. And because these flours don't contain the essential gluten that binds traditional baked goods, many keto baked goods require the addition of naturally derived binding agents, such as guar gum and xanthan gum, to provide the familiar texture that helps make baked treats so delicious and helps hold them together. Other ingredients, such as full-fat dairy and coconut oil, play a key role in adding richness, texture, and sufficient levels of fat to ensure that the recipes not only are delicious but are compliant with the macro ratios necessary to keep your body in a state of ketosis.

All these changes may make you wonder if it's worth the effort, but you'll soon discover that keto desserts are not only delicious, but in most cases, they are very similar in taste and texture to their traditional counterparts. And while keto desserts can contain a high number of calories, they're also low carb and sugar free, so they will still keep your body in a fat-burning state.

UNDERSTANDING GLYCEMIC INDEX, GLYCEMIC LOAD, AND INSULIN

When it comes to the ketogenic diet, it's important to understand glycemic index (GI) and glycemic load (GL), how they apply to the foods we eat, and how they impact our bodies. Glycemic index is a measure of the impact any given food has on our blood sugar levels. Every food is ranked on the GI index scale, which rates foods on a scale of 1 to 100, based on the impact they have on blood sugar. Foods that are higher on the GI scale generally contain higher levels of carbohydrates and sugar, which means they are more quickly digested by the body. In turn, they release higher levels of glucose (sugar) into the bloodstream, which the body then uses for energy. Any glucose that goes unused during the digestion process is then converted into stored fat. High-GI foods can cause the body to add fat because the body is unable to utilize the excess glucose. Low-GI foods, on the other hand, contain fewer carbs and sugar, are digested more slowly by the body, and release glucose into the bloodstream at a much slower rate than high-GI foods. Fewer carbs and sugars mean there's less unused glucose left in the body that can then be converted to fat.

Glycemic load is a bit different than glycemic index and instead measures the total quantity of carbohydrates contained within a certain food, along with the total amount of insulin required by the body to regulate blood sugar levels when the food is digested. This reaction is also known as the *glycemic response*. Unlike the glycemic index, glycemic load does not factor in speed of digestion, but GL is important to understand as it can have a direct impact on the amount of insulin released in the body. Insulin, which is produced by your pancreas, is the master switch that tells your body to either burn fat or store fat, and if you have high levels of insulin circulating in your body as a result of consuming high-GI foods, your body will be in a constant state of fat storage. Additionally, you'll be more at risk of developing serious health conditions, including type 2 diabetes and coronary artery disease. When your GL is low and you're consuming foods that do not trigger a high insulin response, your body no longer needs to rely on carbohydrates as a primary source of energy, which can then trigger your body to access stored fat for energy.

When you're following a ketogenic diet, it's important to keep your glycemic load low by consuming low-GI foods. Carefully managing both of these components is key to burning fat and sustaining ketosis, while still maintaining critical muscle mass.

Using Nut Flours

At the foundation of many keto baked goods are nut flours, which are the essential low-carb replacements for the high-carb wheat flour that is typically used in traditional baking.

WHY USE NUT FLOURS?

Plain wheat flour is the foundation for most traditional baked desserts and treats. So why is it bad for you? While it's inexpensive and very effective for baking, wheat flour is also very high in carbs and often can contribute to multiple serious health issues, including obesity, heart disease, celiac disease, and diabetes.

Nut flours, on the other hand, are very low in carbohydrates and don't elicit a strong glycemic response in the body, which means the body is more inclined to stay in ketosis and burn fat for fuel, as opposed to using sugars for fuel. If you're eating keto and your goal is to stay in a fat-burning state, replacing wheat flour with nut flours in your baked goods is an essential first step, and there are several excellent nut flour options to choose from.

ALMOND FLOUR

Many of the recipes in this book utilize almond flour as a foundation. When combined with a binding agent, items made with almond flour, such as cakes and cookies, bake in a way that is very similar to wheat flour but without the high glycemic response.

Almond flour is made by grinding raw, skinless almonds into a texture that is similar to wheat flour but slightly more course. Almonds can't be ground to the same particle size as regular wheat flour due to the high fat content, otherwise they can turn into a paste. Almond flour can usually be found in the baking aisle in your local supermarket, but you also can make your own by blanching raw almonds, removing the skins, and grinding them in a food processor. Also, almond flour can easily turn rancid, so it should be stored in a cool dry place, such as the vegetable crisper in the fridge.

When using almond flour in recipes, it can be substituted for regular wheat flour at a 1:1 ratio, just as long as a binding agent, such as xanthan gum or guar gum, is used. The amount of binding agent used in recipes will vary depending on the specific recipe, but as a general rule, you'll should use ½ teaspoon of binding agent per 1 cup of almond flour.

ALMOND MEAL

Almond meal is manufactured in the same way as almond flour, but the skins are left intact, so it has a slightly darker color and contains more fiber. It also lends a slightly darker color to baked goods, but generally, it adds the same taste and texture.

When using almond meal in recipes, it can be used in the same way as almond flour and substituted for regular wheat flour at a 1:1 ratio, but you will still need to use a binding agent.

COCONUT FLOUR

Coconut flour is utilized in several recipes throughout this book. It's made by grinding dried coconut meat into a fine texture that closely resembles wheat flour. Coconut flour is typically much whiter in color than almond flour or wheat flour.

When using coconut flour for baking, there are some considerations to keep in mind. Coconut flour contains more fiber and absorbs much more liquid than almond flour, so you won't use as much. If you're replacing wheat flour or almond flour with coconut flour in a recipe, you'll only need to use one quarter of the amount of coconut flour, at a ratio of 1:4. Also, coconut flour doesn't contain gluten, so you'll still need to add a binding agent. As a general rule, you will add about

¼ to ½ teaspoon of binding agent for every ¼ cup of coconut flour to replicate the binding properties of wheat flour.

Because of the absorbent properties of coconut flour, it can be a bit more challenging to work with compared to almond flour, so it's often combined with almond flour. Coconut flour does offer two benefits: Because recipes require less coconut flour, the carbohydrate content in baked goods is reduced. Also, coconut flour has the unique quality of absorbing liquid while still producing a light and fluffy texture.

SESAME SEED FLOUR

Those who are allergic to nuts often have a difficult time making keto-friendly sweets and treats, and many of those people may also prefer to avoid coconut. If you have a nut allergy and can't use nut flours, sesame seed flour is a great alternative. Baked items made with sesame seed flour often turn out softer and fluffier than those made with almond flour. And you can make your own sesame seed flour by grinding dried sesame seeds in a coffee grinder or high-speed blender until a flour-like texture is achieved.

Sesame seed flour should be used in the same ratios as almond flour, but it's important to note that you should use volume measures instead of weighted measures, as sesame seed flour is much lighter in weight in comparison to almond flour.

Gluten-free on the package does not mean keto-friendly!

There's often confusion as to which flours truly are suitable to use on a ketogenic diet. Many flours that are labeled "gluten-free," such rice flour, cassava flour, or besan flour, aren't actually keto-friendly. While these flours are indeed gluten-free, they're actually higher in carbohydrates than even regular wheat flour, so they should be avoided at all times.

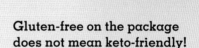

Plain wheat flour has an approximate rating of 75 on the glycemic index, while almond flour has a GI rating of less than 1.

Using Binding Agents

Binding agents give keto baked goods a texture and hold that is similar to those made with wheat flour. And because keto baking uses nut flours, which don't contain gluten, binding agents play an essential role in making desserts that look and taste just like the real thing.

WHY USE BINDING AGENTS?

Gluten is a critical component of baking—it's why pizza dough holds its shape when tossed and why bread rises when it's baked. Gluten acts as the glue between particles of wheat flour to help produce perfect texture and help baked goods retain their shape, so it's a critical component in traditional baking. For those who eat keto, however, eating gluten isn't an option because wheat flour is off limits. Additionally, many people can't digest gluten, which can lead to digestive issues and other potentially serious health problems, particularly for individuals with celiac disease, which is a result of an allergy to gluten. For these reasons, keto followers or those with wheat allergies who are using nut flours to make their desserts also need to use binding agents to produce desirable results.

XANTHAN GUM

Although it does not ferment in its purest form, xanthan gum is a natural substance made by a process of fermentation, which occurs when certain sugars are digested by bacteria and xanthan gum is excreted as a by-product. Xanthan gum is a must-have ingredient for low-carb baking because it helps hold ingredients together to create a bread-like texture that is superior to the crumbly texture common to many gluten-free breads.

Similar to gluten, xanthan gum makes bread rise because it traps gas bubbles and allows them to increase in size. And while it's not an actual yeast or leavener, it still mimics the basic properties of gluten by making almond flour or coconut flour gummy and sticky, which in turn, helps trap the gas bubbles. When used in baking, xanthan gum will thicken at room temperature, while substances like wheat flour and corn flour will only begin to thicken when heated above 194°F (90°C).

It's important to use a xanthan gum that is gluten-free; many varieties are not gluten free and are actually made from wheat. You usually can find gluten-free xanthan gum at most grocery stores, and it's also available from a variety of online sources. A small amount goes a long way; a recipe should never call for much more than a ½ teaspoon. It should be stored in a cool, dry place, such as the vegetable crisper in the fridge.

A word of caution: If too much xanthan gum is consumed, it can cause digestive issues for some people, so be mindful when adding this ingredient to recipes, and be sure to use only the exact amount that is called for in the method.

GUAR GUM

Guar gum, also known as *guaran*, is made from legumes called guar beans. It's a type of carbohydrate, but because it's used in such small amounts and contains such a high amount of fiber, it's acceptable to use as a binder in ketogenic recipes. Guar gum is also known to be a prebiotic, which means it promotes the growth of good bacteria inside the gut while helping to minimize the growth of harmful bacteria. It may also aid in the treatment of irritable bowel syndrome (IBS).

For baking, guar gum will thicken at room temperature and is used to replace gluten, much like xanthan gum is used. It is, in fact, very similar to xanthan gum in the way it behaves when used in baked goods, so it can be used as a replacement for xanthan gum in an equal 1:1 ratio. Like xanthan gum, guar gum should be stored in a cool, dry place, such as the vegetable crisper in the fridge.

As is the case with xanthan gum, high doses of guar gum can have potentially negative effects on the body, mainly because it can absorb up to ten times its weight in water, so be careful when adding this ingredient to your recipes, and be sure to only use the exact amount specified in the recipe.

GELATIN

Powdered gelatin is very useful for baking cakes or creating custards. The consistency it creates is similar to that of gluten, and it can emulate the starches found in high-carb thickeners, such as corn flour or corn starch. Gelatin is derived from the collagen in animal bones, so in addition to being an excellent binder, it also can be a powerful supplement for joint health.

Gelatin powder is used in keto recipes to help bind ingredients much like xanthan gum and guar gum are used, but in a slightly different way. When used in baking—and especially when paired with nut flours, such as almond flour and coconut flour—it can retain moisture and produce a structure that is very similar to a regular cake baked with wheat flour. Additionally, it can be used to thicken substances like puddings and custards. But do note that unlike some other binders or thickeners, it will only thicken once it's cooled (similar to how the collagen from cooked bones will thicken once cooled).

AGAR AGAR

Agar agar is a jelly-like substance made from *agarose* and *agaropectin*, or what's more commonly known as red algae. For those who are vegan or vegetarian, agar agar can be used as a direct replacement for gelatin, which is not vegan or vegetarian friendly. This binding ingredient isn't used in the recipes in this book, but it is suggested as an alternative for those who prefer not to consume gelatin. Agar agar is typically sold as dried strips or in powder form and is particularly useful for thickening puddings, jellies, and custards.

PSYLLIUM HUSK POWDER

Psyllium husk powder is made by grinding the fibrous seed husks from the plant species *plantago ovata*. It's particularly useful for use as a binding agent in baked goods recipes that require a lighter and fluffier texture, but it must be combined with hot water in order to be activated. When activated, it produces a gelatinous substance that can serve as an effective replacement for the gluten present in regular wheat flour. Psyllium husk powder is particularly useful when used as a binder in recipes that require a lighter, airier texture, such as keto bread rolls or éclairs.

Using Sweeteners

The rise of the ketogenic diet has resulted in an abundance of new sweetener options coming onto the market. These new options have also created a lot of confusion as to which truly are acceptable for keto. So which sweeteners can you use, and which should you avoid?

KETO-FRIENDLY SWEETENERS

There are a lot of sweeteners that claim to be keto-friendly, but these are the best options to consider when creating keto-friendly sweets.

Stevia

Stevia rebaudiana (and the active compounds inside the leaves of the stevia plant called *stevia glycosides*) is 150 times sweeter than sugar. Stevia is not digested by the body and has a GI value of zero, which means it will help keep you in a fat-burning state. Stevia not only has a highly sweet taste, but it also can trigger an antibacterial benefit in the body.

Stevia is heat stable, which makes it perfect for baking, but it's used a little differently than sugar. Because it's 150 times sweeter than sugar, you'll use a lot less of it than you would with sugar. The exact ratios you'll use will differ from recipe to recipe, but it's best to follow the guidelines outlined in the products you purchase, because they generally will give you an effective sweetness-to-sugar ratio for whichever brand you use. Stevia can come in granular or liquid form. Liquid stevia, or stevia extract, is best when it's combined with erythritol, because plain stevia extract can actually be relatively bitter. Stevia extract is commonly sold in small dropper bottles, so all stevia extract measurements in the recipes in this book are reflected in drops.

Monk Fruit

Monk fruit is a natural sweetener that is most commonly sold in a liquid form but is also available in a granular form. Also known as Buddha fruit, or longevity fruit, monk fruit has been used for centuries in traditional Chinese medicine (TCM) and is recognized as generally safe by the FDA. The compounds in monk fruit also are believed to have powerful anti-inflammatory properties, and they may help regulate blood sugar levels.

Much like stevia, monk fruit is not digested by the body and does not have a significant impact on insulin or produce a significant blood glucose response, so it can be effective for keeping the body in a fat-burning zone. However, because it's only about 70 percent as sweet as sugar, using a monk fruit sweetener requires making some adjustments in measurements. And because it's a concentrated sweetener that's derived from a natural source, the conversion ratios to sugar can vary slightly from product to product. Be sure to refer to the conversion charts on the products you purchase to ensure your conversions are accurate.

Erythritol

Erythritol is a sugar alcohol. Sugar alcohols are byproducts of the natural fermentation process in foods and can be found in small amounts in fruits and vegetables as well as in fermented products like wine. Commercially manufactured erythritol is created by a certain type of yeast that ferments starches into a sugar alcohol.

Erythritol is believed to be the only sugar alcohol that does not have an impact on blood sugar levels, and is the primary sweetener used throughout this book. It bakes and behaves in a way that is very similar to sugar and it tastes almost identical to sugar. The benefits of using erythritol in baked goods far exceeds those of stevia and monk fruit, mainly because it has so many characteristics that are similar to sugar: It melts the same, tastes very similar, and combines with other ingredients in a very similar way.

There are two varieties of erythritol used in this book. Granular erythritol has a texture similar to common sugar and is ideal for use in recipes where the ingredients are being heated, such as cakes, pies, or cookies. Powdered or confectioners erythritol is ideal for recipes where heat is not used in the preparation and a finer texture is desired for things like cake frostings, puddings, and confections. Look for pure erythritol that is naturally derived and GMO free.

Erythritol is only 70 percent as sweet as sugar, but it contains only 6 percent of the calories and does not impact blood glucose in any significant way. Note that since erythritol is only about 70 percent as sweet as sugar, you'll need to use about 30 percent more in your recipes to achieve a 1:1 ratio with sugar.

Many studies have been done on the prolonged use of erythritol as a sweetener, and the general consensus is that it's a safe food additive. It can, however, cause some digestive issues for some people (particularly those who are sensitive to FODMAPS) because most of the substance does not get digested, which means it can sit in the digestive tract, absorb water, and slightly ferment. For most people, however, this is not an issue.

Also, note that there are some sugar alcohols to avoid, including maltitol, sorbitol, and xylitol, all of which can have an impact on blood sugar levels. (Note that xylitol, in particular, can be toxic for dogs.)

Glycerin

Glycerin is commonly sold in the form of liquid sweeteners called *polyols*, which may also include undesirable sugar alcohols. Glycerin is only about 60 percent as sweet as sugar, so some conversions are required in recipes. While it's not an ideal option for use in keto recipes, it is regarded as generally safe to use and is not believed to impact blood glucose levels.

Sweeteners to Avoid

Sugar comes in many different names and forms, and some companies have become very good at hiding sugars in foods by using different names to disguise the fact that their products contain high GI sweeteners. Here's a comprehensive list of sweeteners that can cause your body to flip that insulin switch and store fat. (You should avoid these at all times.)

agave nectar	date sugar	icing sugar
barley malt	demerara	invert sugar
beet sugar	dextrin	lactose
blackstrap molasses	dextrose	malt syrup
brown rice syrup	diastatic malt	maltodextrin
brown sugar	ethyl maltol	maltose
buttered syrup	evaporated cane juice	maple syrup
cane juice crystals	Florida crystals	molasses
cane sugar	fructose	muscovado
caramel	fruit juice	panela
carob syrup	fruit juice concentrate	raw sugar
castor sugar	glucose	refiners syrup
coconut sugar	glucose solids	rice syrup
confectioners sugar	golden sugar	sorghum syrup
corn syrup	golden syrup	sucanat
corn syrup solids	grape sugar	sucrose
	high fructose corn syrup	sugar
	honey	treacle
		turbinado
		yellow sugar

Many manufacturers create sweetener blends by combining erythritol with stevia or monk fruit, and in some cases, combining erythritol with artificial sweeteners, or even sugar. These blends can produce undesirable results when making keto recipes and often can result in the recipes not being keto friendly. Many baked recipes, such as cookies, won't flatten unless pure erythritol is used in the recipe, so be sure to carefully read the ingredients of any sweetener blend that is labeled as "keto-friendly" to ensure there aren't any undesirable ingredients. For most of the recipes in this book, only pure erythritol is used.

The Keto Kitchen

Making keto sweets requires a slightly different approach for some recipes, but for the most part, many of the techniques, tools, and ingredients are the same as they would be for traditional recipes. Here are some tips, equipment, and ingredients to keep in mind.

HELPFUL TIPS

Here are a few best practices to follow in the kitchen that will help you create keto desserts that come out perfectly every time.

When tempering liquids...

Tempering is just a fancy word for slowly combining, while continuously mixing, two ingredients that are at different temperatures. It helps ensure that a sudden change in temperature doesn't affect the finished texture of the ingredients. Pouring hot milk into a bowl with egg yolks can cause the egg yolks to cook too quickly and become curdled, but very slowly pouring the hot milk into the egg yolks while vigorously whisking the ingredients will help the egg yolks thicken the ingredients, while still keeping the yolks in a liquid state. Tempering is particularly useful when creating custards, ice creams, or anything else that contains egg yolks.

When making whipped cream or meringue...

Making meringue or whipped cream can be tricky. If the conditions aren't right, the egg whites can collapse. Always use a metal or glass bowl, but never use a plastic bowl, because the material can prevent the egg whites from properly whipping. Make sure the bowl is completely clean and free of any moisture, fat, or grease. Always use fresh egg whites and not egg whites from a carton, and make sure the egg whites are at room temperature and not cold (warmer egg whites will create fluffier peaks). Most recipes will call for either stiff or soft peaks. Stiff peaks should stand up against gravity when the mixer is removed from the bowl; soft peaks should sink back into the bowl but not collapse.

When combining whipped ingredients...

When combining an ingredient with another ingredient that has been whipped, it's important to maintain the air inside the whipped ingredient. Combining the ingredients too vigorously can force the air from the whipped ingredient, which can change the texture of the finished product and also cause ingredients like whipped creams and meringues to collapse if they aren't carefully combined. To ensure that the ingredients maintain the proper structure, gently fold the whipped ingredient into the other ingredients by using a gentle stroking motion using a soft, flexible spatula to pull the ingredients upward from the bottom of the bowl. This will prevent the whipped ingredient from losing air while still combining the ingredients.

BASIC EQUIPMENT

Here are some essential items used for the recipes in this book. While most recipes call for a specific size, other sizes may be substituted, if needed.

Springform cake pans are useful for making recipes like cheesecakes, particularly because the bases of keto cheesecakes are made with nut flours and are susceptible to sticking and breaking. To help minimize sticking, I line the base of the pan with parchment paper before locking the ring in place; once the spring is locked, I line the sides with an additional strip of paper before trimming the excess paper from the top edge. (I use this trick with all my cheesecake recipes.) Look for sturdy stainless steel models with a nonstick coating in 8-inch (20.5cm) or 9.5-inch (24cm) sizes.

Loaf pans are handy when making smaller-quantity recipes as well as for recipes like ice creams, tiramisu, or other elongated desserts. Look for sturdy, nonstick pans in 4.5 x 8-inch (11.5 x 20.5cm) or 5 x 9-inch (12.5 x 23cm) sizes.

Square brownie and bar pans are useful when making brownies and bars; their uniform sizes help create equal-sized bars. Look for high-quality pans with thick metal bases that will heat evenly without warping; look for 8 x 8-inch (20.5 x 20.5cm) or 9 x 9-inch (23 x 23cm) sizes.

Pie and tart pans are must-haves for creating perfect pies and tarts. A tart pan can come in handy because the bases of tarts are generally more difficult to remove from pie pans. Look for nonstick models in 8-inch (20.5cm), 8.5-inch (21.5cm), 9-inch (23cm), and 10-inch (25.5cm) sizes.

Baking trays and cake pans are critical for recipes like cookies and cakes. Good quality trays and pans will disperse heat more evenly and will be less susceptible to warping than cheaper options. Look for large baking trays in 26 x 18-inch (66 x 45cm) sizes and square cake pans in 8 x 8-inch (20.5 x 20.5cm) or 9 x 9-inch (23 x 23cm) sizes and 8-inch (20.5cm) round sizes.

An ice cream maker isn't critical to own—and most recipes in this book do include instructions for making the recipes without one—but they can make the process much easier. I utilize a very inexpensive model, because the more expensive versions are not always worth the extra money unless you're making ice cream frequently.

A piping bag can give you accuracy and control when piping icing onto cupcakes or piping filling into desserts like éclairs. If you don't have a piping bag, you can make your own by simply filling a large, sealable freezer bag mostly full with the ingredients, sealing the bag shut, and twisting the top to force the ingredients into one corner of the bag. Use scissors to cut away one corner of the bag, and pipe the ingredients as you would with a piping bag.

OTHER USEFUL INGREDIENTS

Some recipes in this book utilize ingredients that you may be less familiar with. Here are a few that you might want to keep on hand.

- **Cacao nibs** are small bits of the cacao bean that have been minimally processed; they can add an intense flavor to chocolate recipes.
- **Citric acid powder** has a variety of uses, but mostly it's used to add a tart taste and to help balance the sweetness in some desserts; it's sold in bags and can be found in most grocery stores.
- **Cocoa butter** is a high-fat butter extracted from the cocoa bean; it has a pleasant cocoa flavor and aroma, and adds fat and flavor to recipes.
- **Coconut flakes** are large, dried coconut flakes that are larger than shredded coconut and provide a meatier coconut texture to recipes.
- **Coconut oil** is coconut oil that is minimally refined and retains some of the stronger coconut taste; it's sold in a solid state and is packaged in jars.
- **Desiccated coconut** is dried and finely grated coconut meat that can add texture to recipes; it's ideal for coating treats like fat bombs.
- **Refined coconut oil** is coconut oil that has been refined to remove some of the impurities, as well as the stronger coconut taste; it's sold in a solid state and is packaged in jars.
- **Sea salt flakes** are simply a different form of salt that have a more delicate, plate-like structure; they're used for decorating and adding a light touch of salt.
- **Unsweetened canned coconut cream** is thicker than coconut water and is a good dairy-free substitute for heavy cream.
- **Vanilla bean paste** is similar to vanilla extract but has a thicker consistency and contains flecks of vanilla bean.

CHAPTER 2

Cakes, Cupcakes, and Muffins

Virtually anything that can be baked can be made keto.
This chapter features fluffy cakes, rich and creamy
cheesecakes, cupcakes, tiramisu, donuts, and more.

GLUTEN FREE ⊛ SUGAR FREE

Vanilla Cake with Fresh Berries

This extraordinary cake is topped with a cream cheese icing and fresh berries, and is perfect for celebrating birthdays or special occasions with friends, family, and loved ones.

PREP TIME: **15 MINUTES**	COOK TIME: **45 MINUTES**	PASSIVE TIME: **30 MINUTES**

MAKES: 8 SERVINGS
SERVING SIZE: 1 SLICE

For the cake

1 cup (3.2oz/100g) almond flour

¼ cup (1oz /30g) coconut flour

1 tsp baking powder

¼ tsp salt

½ cup (3.2oz/100g) granular erythritol

5 large eggs, separated

¼ cup (2oz/60g) heavy whipping cream

½ cup (3.2oz/100g) unsalted butter, melted

1 tsp vanilla extract

½ tbsp powdered gelatin

1 tbsp warm water

For topping

1¼ cups (10oz/285g) full-fat cream cheese

2 tbsp heavy whipping cream

3 tbsp confectioners erythritol

2 tsp vanilla extract

2 tsp lemon juice

½ cup (5oz/150g) fresh blueberries

½ cup (5.1oz/160g) fresh strawberries, thinly sliced

1. Preheat the oven to 320°F (160°C) and line an 8-inch (20cm) round cake pan with parchment paper.

2. In a medium bowl, combine the almond flour, coconut flour, baking powder, salt, and erythritol. Mix until the ingredients are well combined and a uniform color is achieved. Set aside.

3. In a separate medium bowl, beat the egg whites with a hand mixer until soft peaks form. Set aside.

4. In a third medium bowl, combine the egg yolks, whipping cream, melted butter, and vanilla extract. Whisk to combine. Set aside.

5. In a small bowl, combine the gelatin and warm water. Stir until the gelatin is completely dissolved, then add to the egg yolk mixture. Stir.

6. Carefully fold the egg yolk mixture into the egg white mixture, then fold the almond flour mixture into the egg mixture. Pour the batter into the prepared cake pan. Transfer to the oven and bake for 45 minutes.

7. While the cake is baking, make the icing by combining the cream cheese, whipping cream, and erythritol in a medium bowl. Stir, then add the vanilla extract and lemon juice. Continue stirring until a smooth, creamy texture is achieved.

8. When a toothpick inserted into the middle of the cake comes out clean, remove from the oven and set aside to cool for 20 minutes.

9. Once the cake is cooled, slice in half lengthwise. Cover the first half with one third of the icing and top with half the berries. Place the other half on top of the base, spread the remaining icing over the entire surface of the cake, then top with the remaining berries. Cut into 8 equal-sized servings. Store in an airtight container in the fridge for up to 5 days.

Tip Blueberries and strawberries are interchangeable with blackberries and raspberries.

NUTRITION PER SERVING	//	261 CALORIES	//	24g TOTAL FAT	//	6.5g TOTAL CARBS	//	4g NET CARBS	//	7g PROTEIN

Ⓢ **NUT FREE** Ⓖ **GLUTEN FREE** Ⓢ **SUGAR FREE**

Flourless Chocolate Cake

This light and airy cake combines creamy chocolate with
just a few additional ingredients to make a simple dessert
that will satisfy even the pickiest chocolate lover.

| PREP TIME: **15 MINUTES** | COOK TIME: **45 MINUTES** | PASSIVE TIME: **1 HOUR** |

MAKES: 8 SERVINGS
SERVING SIZE: 1 SLICE

1 tsp butter (for greasing)

7oz (200g) unsweetened dark
chocolate, chopped

⅓ cup (2.8oz/80g) unsalted butter,
diced

½ tsp salt

6 large eggs, separated

1 cup (4.5oz/130g) granular
erythritol

1. Preheat the oven to 275°F (135°C) and coat the interior of an 8-inch springform pan with 1 teaspoon butter.

2. In a medium glass bowl, combine the chocolate and butter. Microwave on high for 90 seconds, stirring every 30 seconds, until the ingredients are melted. Add the salt and stir. Set aside to cool.

3. In a medium bowl, beat the egg whites until stiff peaks form, then slowly add the erythritol and continue mixing until the erythritol is completely dissolved.

4. Once the chocolate and butter mixture has cooled completely, add the egg yolks. Whisk to combine.

5. Pour the chocolate into the middle of the egg whites. Use a spatula to gently fold the chocolate into the egg whites.

6. Pour the cake mixture into the prepared pan. Place the pan on the middle oven rack and bake for 50 minutes, checking the doneness after 40 minutes by inserting a toothpick into the middle of the cake. If the toothpick comes out clean, remove the cake from the oven and let it cool completely before cutting into 8 equal-sized servings. Store in an airtight container in the fridge for up to 5 days, or freeze for up to 3 weeks.

Tip If the top becomes cracked, you can sift confectioners erythritol over top or lightly spread whipped cream over the top of the cake.

| **NUTRITION PER SERVING** | 257 CALORIES | 25g TOTAL FAT | 9g TOTAL CARBS | 5g NET CARBS | 4g PROTEIN |

GLUTEN FREE SUGAR FREE

Pumpkin Cheesecake

The delicious secret to this cheesecake lies in the combination of the pumpkin-spiced base, which is made from ground walnuts, and the pumpkin pie spice-infused filling, which is slightly sweet and very creamy.

PREP TIME: **15 MINUTES**　　　COOK TIME: **1 HOUR**　　　PASSIVE TIME: **1 HR 30 MINS**

MAKES: 12 SERVINGS
SERVING SIZE: 1 SLICE

For the base

1 tsp butter (for greasing)

1½ cups (14.8oz/420g) finely ground walnuts

¼ cup (1.8oz /50g) butter, melted

2 tbsp granular erythritol

½ tsp pumpkin pie spice

1 large egg white

For the filling

2 cups (17.5oz/500g) full-fat cream cheese, warmed to room temperature

¾ cup (6oz/170g) heavy whipping cream

½ cup (3oz/90g) granular erythritol

½ cup (3oz/90g) canned sugar-free pumpkin purée

½ tsp pumpkin pie spice

1 tsp vanilla extract

3 large eggs, warmed to room temperature

1. Preheat the oven to 320°F (160°C) and grease an 8-inch (20cm) springform cake pan with 1 teaspoon butter.

2. In a medium bowl, combine the ground walnuts, melted butter, erythritol, pumpkin pie spice, and the egg white. Mix until well combined.

3. Add the walnut base to the prepared cake pan and press the mixture into the bottom and sides of the pan. Transfer to the oven to bake for 10 minutes, then set aside to cool.

4. Make the filling by combining the cream cheese, heavy whipping cream, erythritol, pumpkin purée, pumpkin pie spice, and vanilla extract in a large bowl. Mix well, then add the eggs, one at a time; mix to combine, making sure to mix the ingredients well before adding each additional egg.

5. Pour the filling mixture into the cake pan. Wrap the bottom and sides of the pan in aluminum foil, and place the pan in a large baking pan filled half full with water. This will help prevent the cheesecake from drying out, and also help prevent the top of the cheesecake from cracking.

6. Bake for 1 hour, then promptly turn off the oven, crack the oven door, and let the cheesecake cool in the oven for 30 minutes. Transfer to the fridge to set for 1 additional hour, then cut into 12 equal-sized slices. Store in an airtight container in the fridge for up to 5 days.

Tip If you don't have pumpkin spice, you can combine ½ tsp ground cinnamon, ¼ tsp ground ginger, and ¼ tsp grated nutmeg. If you can't find pumpkin purée, you can substitute an equal amount of steamed, mashed pumpkin.

NUTRITION PER SERVING	470 CALORIES	47g TOTAL FAT	7g TOTAL CARBS	5g NET CARBS	10g PROTEIN

⊗ NUT FREE ⊛ GLUTEN FREE ⊗ SUGAR FREE

Pavlova

This dessert was named for a Russian ballerina and features a deliciously light and fluffy meringue covered in cream and fruit. This is my healthier take on a recipe that was passed down to me from my late grandmother.

PREP TIME: **15 MINUTES**	COOK TIME: **1 HR 30 MINS**	PASSIVE TIME: **20 MINUTES**

MAKES: 6 SERVINGS
SERVING SIZE: 1 SLICE

For the meringue

6 large egg whites, warmed to room temperature

½ cup (2.8oz/80g) confectioners erythritol

1 tsp vanilla extract

½ tsp xanthan gum

1 tsp cream of tartar

For the topping

½ cup (4fl oz/120ml) heavy whipping cream

¼ cup (2.5oz/75g) fresh blueberries

¼ cup (2.8oz/80g) fresh strawberries, thinly sliced

1. Preheat the oven to 390°F (200°C) and line a large baking sheet with parchment paper.

2. Add the egg whites to a large glass mixing bowl. Using a hand mixer, beat on high for 2 minutes or until stiff peaks form. Be very careful to only beat the egg whites just until stiff peaks form, otherwise they may collapse.

3. Add the erythritol, vanilla extract, xanthan gum, and cream of tartar. Using a rubber spatula, carefully fold until the ingredients are well combined but the mixture still appears light and fluffy.

4. Using a spatula, evenly spread the meringue onto the parchment paper and into a circular shape. Transfer to the oven and immediately reduce the oven temperature to 215°F (100°C). Bake for 90 minutes or until the edges begin to lightly brown, then turn off the oven, crack the oven door, and let the meringue cool in the oven for a minimum of 20 minutes.

5. While the meringue is cooling, add the heavy cream to a medium glass bowl. Using a hand mixer, beat on high until soft peaks form.

6. Once the meringue is cooled, use a spoon to spread the whipped cream over top, then place the blueberries and strawberry slices in an even layer on top. Cut into 6 equal-sized servings and serve promptly (this dessert is best served fresh and will not keep in the fridge).

Tip For best results, use a glass mixing bowl and not a metal or plastic bowl. Also, make sure there are no egg yolks in the mixture because this can ruin the meringue.

NUTRITION PER SERVING	121 CALORIES	10g TOTAL FAT	4g TOTAL CARBS	3g NET CARBS	4.5g PROTEIN

GLUTEN FREE **SUGAR FREE**

Macadamia Nut Cupcakes

Macadamia nuts make the perfect pairing with this delicious
cupcake recipe. Not only are they sugar free, but they
will keep your sweet tooth satisfied and help keep
you feeling full with a bounty of healthy fats.

PREP TIME: **10 MINUTES**	COOK TIME: **20 MINUTES**	PASSIVE TIME: **30 MINUTES**

MAKES: 6
SERVING SIZE: 1

For the cake

1 cup (3.2oz/100g) almond flour

½ cup (2.7oz/80g)
   granular erythritol

1 tsp baking powder

2 tbsp butter, melted

2 tbsp unsweetened almond milk

1 tsp vanilla extract

2 large eggs

¼ cup (1.7oz/50g) unsalted
   macadamia nuts, roughly
   chopped

¼ cup (1.4oz/40g) unsweetened
   cocoa butter buttons, cut into
   quarters

For the icing

½ cup heavy whipping cream
   (3.8fl oz/115ml)

1 tbsp confectioners erythritol

1 tsp vanilla extract

1. Preheat the oven to 355°F (180°C).

2. In a medium bowl, combine the almond flour, erythritol, and baking powder. Stir, then add the melted butter, almond milk, vanilla extract, and eggs. Whisk until well combined.

3. Fold the chopped macadamia nuts and cocoa butter pieces into the mixture.

4. Spoon the mixture into 6 small muffin holders. Transfer to the oven and bake for 20 minutes or until the tops turn golden brown.

5. While the muffins are baking, make the icing by combining the whipping cream, erythritol, and vanilla extract in a medium bowl. Using a hand mixer, whip the ingredients until the mixture doubles in size. Remove the cupcakes from the oven and set aside to cool for 15 minutes.

6. Once the cupcakes are cooled, use a circular motion to pipe the icing over the top of the cupcakes. Store in an airtight container in the fridge for up to 3 days.

Tip For a decorative touch, top with shaved macadamia nuts, extra cocoa butter bits, or desiccated coconut.

NUTRITION PER SERVING	430 CALORIES	43g TOTAL FAT	5.5g TOTAL CARBS	3g NET CARBS	7g PROTEIN

✳ GLUTEN FREE ❀ SUGAR FREE

Simple Sponge Cake

This versatile low-carb sponge cake can be used in a variety of keto dessert recipes. The secret ingredient is the ricotta cheese, which helps create a fluffy, airy texture.

| PREP TIME: **10 MINUTES** | COOK TIME: **40 MINUTES** | COOLING TIME: **1 HOUR** |

MAKES: 6 SERVINGS
SERVING SIZE: 1 SLICE

1 cup (8.5oz/250g) full-fat ricotta cheese

⅓ cup (1.9oz/55g) granular erythritol

3 large eggs

½ cup (4oz/115g) butter, melted

¾ cup (2.5oz/70g) almond flour

1 tsp baking powder

½ tsp salt

1. Preheat the oven to 320°F (160°C), and line a 9 x 9-inch (22 x 22cm) square baking pan with parchment paper.

2. In a medium bowl, combine the ricotta cheese and erythritol. Whisk continuously, adding one egg at a time, until all the eggs are incorporated into the mixture.

3. Add the melted butter, almond flour, baking powder, and salt. Mix until well combined.

4. Pour the mixture into the prepared baking pan and transfer to the oven to bake for 40 minutes, checking the cake every 5 minutes after the 30-minute mark to ensure it doesn't burn.

5. When the cooking time is complete, insert a toothpick into the middle of the cake to test for doneness. If the toothpick comes out clean, remove the cake from the oven and set aside to cool completely before slicing into 6 equal-sized servings. Store in an airtight container in the fridge for up to 5 days.

Tip Make sure to let the cake cool completely before slicing; otherwise it could deflate.

| NUTRITION PER SERVING | 310 CALORIES | 28.5g TOTAL FAT | 4.5g TOTAL CARBS | 3g NET CARBS | 11g PROTEIN |

🥨 **GLUTEN FREE** 🍬 **SUGAR FREE**

Chocolate Chip Muffins

These muffins are a great little on-the-go snack for when you need a sweet little bite to kill those sugar cravings. If you love chocolate chip cookies, you'll love these muffins!

PREP TIME: **10 MINUTES**   COOK TIME: **20 MINUTES**   COOLING TIME: **30 MINUTES**

MAKES: 6
SERVING SIZE: 1

1 tsp butter (for greasing)

1 cup (3.2oz/100g) almond flour

¼ cup (1.2oz/40g) granular erythritol

1 tsp baking powder

2 tbsp butter, melted

2 tbsp unsweetened almond milk

1 tsp vanilla extract

2 large eggs

¼ cup (1.8oz/50g) unsweetened chocolate chips

1. Preheat the oven to 355°F (180°C), and coat a small muffin pan with 1 teaspoon butter.

2. In a large bowl, combine the almond flour, erythritol, and baking powder. Mix well to combine.

3. Add the melted butter, almond milk, vanilla extract, and eggs. Whisk until well combined, then fold the chocolate chips into the batter.

4. Spoon the mixture into 6 small muffin cups and transfer to the oven. Bake for 20 minutes or until the tops turn golden brown. Let cool for a minimum of 30 minutes before serving. Store in an airtight container in the fridge for up to 5 days, or freeze for up to 3 weeks.

Tip You can substitute unsweetened baking chocolate for the chocolate chips. Chop the chocolate into small pieces and insert them into the batter in the cups prior to placing the muffins in the oven.

NUTRITION PER SERVING // 229 CALORIES // 20g TOTAL FAT // 8g TOTAL CARBS // 5g NET CARBS // 7g PROTEIN

🌾 **GLUTEN FREE** 🍬 **SUGAR FREE**

Blueberry Muffins

These delightful muffins are the perfect accompaniment
to your morning coffee or tea, and you'll be getting
the benefits of eating healthy fats while still
satisfying that urge for something sweet!

PREP TIME: **10 MINUTES**   COOK TIME: **20 MINUTES**   PASSIVE TIME: **30 MINUTES**

MAKES: 6
SERVING SIZE: 1

1 cup (3.2oz/100g) almond flour

¼ cup (1.2oz/40g) granular erythritol

1 tsp baking powder

2 tbsp (1oz/30g) butter, melted

2 tbsp (1fl oz/30ml) unsweetened almond milk

1 tsp vanilla extract

2 large eggs

¼ cup (1.1oz/35g) fresh blueberries

1. Preheat the oven to 355°F (180°C), and line a small muffin tin with cupcake liners.

2. In a large bowl, combine the almond flour, erythritol, and baking powder. Stir to combine, then add the melted butter, almond milk, vanilla extract, and eggs. Whisk until well combined.

3. Pour the mixture into 6 small muffin cups. Gently press equal amounts of the blueberries into the top of each muffin.

4. Transfer to the oven and bake for 20 minutes or until the tops turn golden brown. Let cool before serving. Store in an airtight container in the fridge for up to 5 days, or freeze for up to 3 weeks.

Tip If you choose to mix the blueberries into the batter, make sure to include equal amounts of blueberries in each muffin.

NUTRITION PER SERVING	175 CALORIES	15g TOTAL FAT	4g TOTAL CARBS	2g NET CARBS	6g PROTEIN

⊗ **NUT FREE** ⊛ **GLUTEN FREE** ⊛ **SUGAR FREE**

Lemon Coconut Cake with Cream Cheese Icing

This versatile cake is perfect for any occassion; the sweet
cream cheese icing compliments a zesty lemon tang. A few of
my followers have won baking competitions with this recipe!

PREP TIME: **15 MINUTES**	COOK TIME: **1 HOUR**	COOLING TIME: **2 HOURS**

MAKES: 12 SERVINGS
SERVING SIZE: 1 SLICE

For the cake

5 large eggs, separated

½ cup (1.2oz/40g) coconut flour

¼ cup (1.2oz/40g) granular
   erythritol

½ cup (4oz/115g) butter, melted

Juice of ½ lemon

½ tsp lemon zest

½ tsp xanthan gum

½ tsp salt

For the icing

1 cup (8.8oz/250g) full-fat
   cream cheese

3 tbsp confectioners erythritol

1 tsp vanilla extract

½ tsp lemon zest

1. Preheat the oven to 355°F (180°C), and line a 9 x 5-inch (23 x 13cm) loaf pan
   with parchment paper.

2. In a large bowl, beat the egg whites until soft peaks form. Set aside.

3. In a separate large bowl, combine the egg yolks, coconut flour, erythritol,
   melted butter, lemon juice, lemon zest, xanthan gum, and salt. Mix well.
   Use a rubber spatula to gently fold the egg whites into the egg yolk mixture.

4. Pour the cake batter into the prepared pan and transfer to the oven to bake
   for 45 minutes or until a toothpick inserted into the middle of the cake comes
   out clean.

5. While the cake is baking, make the icing by combining the cream cheese,
   erythritol, vanilla extract, and lemon zest in a medium bowl. Stir until the
   ingredients are well combined.

6. When the cake is done baking, evenly spread the icing over the entire
   surface of the cake. Cut into 12 equal-sized servings. Store in an airtight
   container in the fridge for up to 5 days.

Tip For an extra decorative touch, draw a skewer across the top of the cake in a chess
board pattern. (It's an old-fashioned decorating technique I learned from my grandma.)

NUTRITION PER SERVING	188 CALORIES	17g TOTAL FAT	4.2g TOTAL CARBS	2.5g NET CARBS	4.5g PROTEIN

GLUTEN FREE 🌾 SUGAR FREE

Mint Chocolate Cheesecake

If you love the flavor combination of mint and chocolate,
you're going to absolutely love this cheesecake! It takes
a little time to make, but it's worth the effort.

PREP TIME: **30 MINUTES** COOK TIME: **50 MINUTES** PASSIVE TIME: **2 HOURS**

MAKES: 12 SERVINGS
SERVING SIZE: 1 SLICE

For the base

1½ cups (6.2oz/150g) almond flour

½ cup (1.2oz/40g) coconut flour

¼ tsp xanthan gum

½ tsp baking powder

¼ cup (1.2oz/40g)
granular erythritol

¼ tsp salt

½ cup (4.7oz/135g) butter, cold

For the filling

2 x 8oz (17.5oz/500g) blocks
full-fat cream cheese

¾ cup (6oz/170g) full-fat
sour cream

¾ cup (5oz/120g)
granular erythritol

1 tsp peppermint extract

3 large eggs

⅓ cup (1.8oz/50g) unsweetened
baking chocolate, chopped

¼ cup (2fl oz/60ml) heavy cream

1. In a food processor, combine the almond flour, coconut flour, xanthan gum, baking powder, erythritol, and salt. Pulse until combined. Add the cold butter in tablespoon chunks and process for 20 seconds or until the ingredients are just combined.

2. Tightly wrap the base mixture in plastic wrap and transfer to the fridge to chill for a minimum of 2 hours. Preheat the oven to 320°F (160°C), and line a 9.5-inch (24cm) springform pan with parchment paper.

3. Remove the chilled base from the fridge and evenly press the mixture into the bottom and halfway up the sides of the prepared pan. Using a fork, poke holes in the bottom of the base. Transfer to the oven to bake for 15 minutes.

4. While the base is baking, make the filling by combining the cream cheese, sour cream, erythritol, and peppermint extract in a large bowl. Add 1 egg to the bowl and begin mixing the ingredients, adding one egg at a time, until all the eggs are incorporated and the ingredients are well combined.

5. Remove the base the oven and let it cool for 10 minutes. Spoon the filling into the base. Set aside.

6. Place the chocolate in a small heatsafe bowl. In a small saucepan, heat the heavy cream until it just begins to bubble, then pour the hot cream over the chocolate and let it sit for 3 minutes. Stir the mixture until a smooth texture is achieved and no lumps remain. Pour the mixture over the cheesecake filling and use a fork to gently swirl the surface to create a decorative pattern.

7. Wrap the bottom and sides of the pan in aluminum foil, and place the pan in a large baking pan filled half full with water. Transfer to the oven and bake for 45–50 minutes or until a toothpick inserted into the center comes out clean. Promptly turn off the oven, crack the oven door, and let the cheesecake cool in the oven for an additional 30 minutes. Transfer to the fridge to chill for a minimum of 1 hour, then cut into 12 equal-sized slices. Store in an airtight container in the fridge for up to 1 week.

NUTRITION PER SERVING	438 CALORIES	43g TOTAL FAT	7.5g TOTAL CARBS	5g NET CARBS	8.5g PROTEIN

GLUTEN FREE SUGAR FREE EGG FREE

No-Bake Vanilla Cheesecake Pots

Traditional cheesecake can take a lot of time and work to prepare, but these no-bake, single-serving cheesecake pots are incredibly simple to make, and they're also delicious!

PREP TIME: **10 MINUTES**   COOK TIME: **NONE**   PASSIVE TIME: **2 HOURS**

MAKES: 4
SERVING SIZE: 1

¼ cup (4oz/120g) finely ground walnuts

⅓ cup (3oz/90g) full-fat cream cheese

¼ cup (2oz/60g) heavy whipping cream

¼ cup (1oz/30g) keto-friendly vanilla protein powder

3fl oz (90ml) water (about ⅓ cup)

1. Evenly divide the ground walnuts across 4 small jars or cups.

2. In a small mixing bowl, combine the cream cheese, whipping cream, and protein powder. Slowly add the water in small amounts and stir until the texture becomes smooth and creamy but not watery. (The amount of water required may vary depending on the brand of protein powder you're using.)

3. Spoon the cream cheese mixture on top of the walnut base. Cover the pots with plastic wrap and transfer to the fridge to set for a minimum of 2 hours. Serve chilled. Store in the fridge for up to 5 days.

Tip Using a grass-fed, stevia-sweetened protein powder is ideal but not critical; just make sure the protein powder is keto-friendly.

NUTRITION PER SERVING	356 CALORIES	33g TOTAL FAT	6.5g TOTAL CARBS	4.5g NET CARBS	12g PROTEIN

GLUTEN FREE SUGAR FREE

New York-Style Cheesecake

This lightly sweet cheesecake has always been a favorite among my followers. The base layer of this version is very similar to a traditional crust, and the inside is just as creamy and delicious as a traditional cheesecake.

| PREP TIME: **20 MINUTES** | COOK TIME: **50 MINUTES** | PASSIVE TIME: **2 HRS 30 MINS** |

MAKES: 12 SERVINGS
SERVING SIZE: 1 SLICE

For the crust

1½ cups (6.2oz/150g) almond flour

½ cup (1.2oz/40g) coconut flour

¼ tsp xanthan gum

½ tsp baking powder

¼ cup (1.2oz/40g) granular erythritol

¼ tsp salt

½ cup (4.7oz/135g) cold butter

For the filling

17.5oz (500g) full-fat cream cheese

¾ cup (6oz/170g) full-fat sour cream

¾ cup (5oz/120g) granular erythritol

1 tsp vanilla extract

1 tsp freshly-grated lemon zest

3 large eggs

1. Combine the almond flour, coconut flour, xanthan gum, baking powder, erythritol, and salt in a food processor. Pulse until combined.

2. Add the butter in tablespoon chunks. Process for 20 seconds or until the ingredients are just combined.

3. Wrap the dough tightly in plastic wrap and transfer to the fridge to chill for a minimum of 2 hours.

4. Preheat the oven to 320°F (160°C), and line a 9.5-inch (24cm) springform pan with parchment paper.

5. Place the chilled dough between two sheets of parchment paper and roll it out flat enough to cover the bottom of the pan. Line the bottom of the pan with the dough, then use a fork to poke holes in the dough. Transfer to the oven and bake for 15 minutes.

6. While the crust is baking, make the filling by combining the cream cheese, sour cream, erythritol, vanilla extract, and lemon zest in a large bowl. Using a hand mixer, mix the ingredients on medium while adding the eggs, one at a time, and ensuring the ingredients are combined before adding the next egg. Mix until well combined.

7. When the crust is done baking, add the filling to the pan. Wrap the bottom and sides of the pan in aluminum foil and place the pan in a large baking pan filled half full with water. Transfer to the oven and bake for 50 minutes or until a toothpick inserted in the middle comes out clean.

8. Turn off the oven and crack the oven door, but leave the cheesecake in the oven to slowly cool for 30 additional minutes. Transfer the cheesecake to the fridge to chill and set for a minimum of one hour before slicing into 12 equal-sized servings. Store covered in an airtight container in the fridge for up to 5 days.

| NUTRITION PER SERVING | 347 CALORIES | 33g TOTAL FAT | 7g TOTAL CARBS | 5g NET CARBS | 7.g PROTEIN |

🌾 **GLUTEN FREE** 🍬 **SUGAR FREE**

Tiramisu

This keto version of a classic Italian dessert features an alcohol-infused base and a creamy mascarpone cheese filling. Your entire family will love this recipe!

PREP TIME: **30 MINUTES**	COOK TIME: **25 MINUTES**	PASSIVE TIME: **4 HOURS**

MAKES: 10 SERVINGS
SERVING SIZE: 1 SLICE

For the base

1 tsp butter (for greasing)
½ cup (50g/1.8oz) almond flour
1 tbsp coconut flour
½ tsp powdered gelatin
½ tsp baking powder
⅓ cup (1.8oz/50g) granular erythritol
2 large eggs
½ tsp vanilla extract
2 tbsp heavy whipping cream

For the soaking liquor

¼ cup (2fl oz/60ml) heavy whipping cream
¼ cup granular erythritol
¼ cup (2fl oz/60ml) vodka (optional)
1 tsp instant espresso powder

For the filling

½ cup (3.8fl oz/115ml) heavy whipping cream
1 cup (8.8oz/250g) full-fat mascarpone cheese
1 large egg yolk
1 tsp vanilla extract
¼ cup (1.2oz/40g) granular erythritol
1 tbsp unsweetened cocoa powder (for dusting)

1. Preheat the oven to 355°F (180°C), and grease a 8.5 x 5-in (21.5 x 12.5cm) loaf pan with 1 teaspoon butter.

2. Make the base by combining the almond flour, coconut flour, gelatin, baking powder, and erythritol in a large bowl. Mix until well combined.

3. Add the eggs, vanilla extract, and whipping cream. Mix until well combined, then transfer the mixture to the prepared pan. Bake for 25 minutes or until a toothpick inserted into the middle comes out clean. Remove from the oven and set aside to cool.

4. While the base is baking, make the soaking liquor by combining the whipping cream, erythritol, vodka (if using), and espresso powder in a small saucepan placed over low heat. Stirring frequently, heat until the erythritol and espresso powder are completely dissolved. Set aside to cool.

5. Make the filling by adding the whipping cream to a large glass bowl. Using a hand mixer, beat the cream on high until stiff peaks form. Add the mascarpone cheese, egg yolk, vanilla extract, and erythritol. Use a rubber spatula to carefully fold the ingredients together.

6. Pour the soaking liquor over the base and let it soak in for 2 minutes. Spread the filling over the top, then dust the top with the cocoa powder.

7. Cover the pan with plastic wrap and transfer to the fridge to set for a minimum of 4 hours. Serve promptly, or cover with plastic wrap and store in the fridge for up to 5 days.

Tip If you want additional layers, slice the base layer horizontally into 2 parts prior to soaking. Divide the filling between the two sections.

NUTRITION PER SERVING	251 CALORIES	23g TOTAL FAT	4g TOTAL CARBS	2.5g NET CARBS	4.5g PROTEIN

Ⓧ **NUT FREE** Ⓖ **GLUTEN FREE** Ⓢ **SUGAR FREE**

Cinnamon Doughnuts

These donuts are the perfect sweet treat! They're sugar-free,
gluten-free, and nut-free (because coconut is considered
a drupe), so this means they're also guilt-free! And they're
quicker to make than you might expect.

PREP TIME: **15 MINUTES** | COOK TIME: **10 MINUTES** | PASSIVE TIME: **5 MINUTES**

MAKES: 10
SERVING SIZE: 1

½ cup coconut oil

For the batter

½ cup (4oz/115ml) full-fat
sour cream

¼ cup (2fl oz/60ml) heavy
whipping cream

¼ cup (1.4oz/40g) granular
erythritol

4 large eggs, warmed to
room temperature

1 tsp vanilla extract

½ cup (1.4oz/40g) coconut flour

¼ tsp ground nutmeg

½ tsp baking powder

¼ tsp salt

For the cinnamon coating

¼ cup (1.4oz/40g) granular
erythritol

1 tsp ground cinnamon

1. Preheat the oven to 355°F (180°C).

2. In a medium bowl, combine the sour cream, whipping cream, erythritol, eggs, and vanilla extract. Mix well, then add the coconut flour, nutmeg, baking powder, and salt. Stir to combine, then let the mixture rest for 5 minutes to allow the coconut flour to absorb the liquid.

3. Using a silicone donut mold or nonstick donut pan, slowly fill the molds three quarters full with the batter. Transfer to the oven and bake for 15 minutes or until the donuts are firm to the touch.

4. While the donuts are baking, make the cinnamon coating by combining the erythritol and cinnamon on a small plate. Mix well and set aside.

5. Remove the donuts from the oven and set aside to cool for 5 minutes, then remove them from the molds.

6. Add the coconut oil to a large frying pan. Heat the oil for 5 minutes or until a few drops of water sizzle in the oil. Place the donuts in the oil and fry for 2 minutes per side or until they turn golden brown.

7. Coat the warm donuts in the cinnamon mixture and transfer to a cooling rack to cool slightly. (These are best eaten fresh but can be stored in an airtight container in the fridge for up to 5 days.)

Tip If you don't have a donut mold or pan, you can cut small strips of parchment paper, shape them into rings, and place them in the centers of muffin cups. Pour the batter into the cups but not inside the rings.

NUTRITION PER SERVING	125 CALORIES	12g TOTAL FAT	1.5g TOTAL CARBS	1g NET CARBS	3g PROTEIN

⊛ **GLUTEN FREE** ⊛ **SUGAR FREE**

Boston Cream Pie

Boston cream pie is actually a cake filled with a custard-like filling. This treat takes a little time to make, but it's divine!

PREP TIME: **20 MINUTES**	COOK TIME: **40 MINUTES**	PASSIVE TIME: **2 HRS 30 MINS**

MAKES: 10 SERVINGS
SERVING SIZE: 1 SLICE

For the cake

1 tbsp butter (for greasing)

1 cup (3.2oz/100g) almond flour

⅓ cup (1oz/30g) coconut flour

1 tsp baking powder

5 large eggs

¼ cup (2fl oz/60ml) heavy whipping cream

⅔ cup (3.2oz/100g) granular erythritol

½ cup (3.2oz/100g) butter, warmed to room temperature

1 tsp vanilla extract

½ tsp powdered gelatin

1 tbsp warm water

For the filling and ganache

¾ cup (8.5fl oz/250ml) unsweetened almond milk

½ cup (4fl oz/120ml) heavy whipping cream

2 tbsp granular erythritol

2 tsp vanilla extract

1 tsp powdered gelatin

1 tbsp butter

⅓ cup (2.8fl oz/80ml) heavy whipping cream

1.8oz (50g) 90% dark chocolate, diced

1 tbsp granular erythritol

⅛ tsp salt

1. Preheat the oven to 355°F (180°C), and coat an 8-inch (20cm) round cake pan with 1 tablespoon butter.

2. In a medium bowl, combine the almond flour, coconut flour, and baking powder. Stir to combine. In a separate medium bowl, combine the eggs, whipping cream, erythritol, butter, and vanilla extract. Whisk until combined. In a third medium bowl, combine the gelatin and water, and stir until the gelatin is dissolved. Add the egg mixture to the gelatin mixture. Stir.

3. Using a spatula, fold the dry ingredients into the wet ingredients. Pour the batter into the prepared cake pan. Transfer to the oven and bake for 40 minutes or until the center of the cake is firm. Set aside to cool.

4. While the cake is baking, make the custard filling by combining the almond milk, whipping cream, erythritol, vanilla extract, gelatin, and butter in a medium saucepan placed over low heat. Cook for 5 minutes, then transfer the mixture to a large bowl, cover, and transfer to the fridge to cool for 2 hours, stirring after 1 hour.

5. Once the cake has cooled, use a large, sharp knife to cut the cake sideways and into two equal halves. Remove the top half of the cake, being careful not to break it. Set aside.

6. Once the custard filling has thickened, spread it over the middle of the bottom section of the cake, keeping 1 inch (2.5cm) of room around the circumference of the cake to ensure the top doesn't push the custard out of the cake. Place the top half of the cake on top of the bottom half.

7. Make the chocolate ganache by adding the whipping cream to a heatproof bowl and heating in the microwave for 1 minute. Add the chocolate to the bowl and let it sit for 2 minutes; begin stirring the chocolate mixture continuously while adding the erythritol and salt. Continue stirring until the ingredients are completely incorporated.

8. Drizzle the ganache over top of the cake and transfer to the fridge to chill for 2 hours before serving. Store in the fridge for up to 4 days.

NUTRITION PER SERVING	//	315 CALORIES	//	29g TOTAL FAT	//	6g TOTAL CARBS	//	3.5g NET CARBS	//	7.5g PROTEIN

CHAPTER 3

Puddings and Custards

Creamy puddings and velvety custards are never off limits
on keto! Here, you'll find recipes for everything from
crème brûlée, to chocolate mousse, to bread pudding.

DAIRY FREE ● GLUTEN FREE ● SUGAR FREE

Custard

Traditional custard is made with milk, eggs, sugar, and cornstarch, which means it's loaded with carbs. This custard contains very few carbs, tastes fantastic, and is way easier to make than traditional custard!

| PREP TIME: **5 MINUTES** | COOK TIME: **20 MINUTES** | PASSIVE TIME: **NONE** |

MAKES: 4 SERVINGS
SERVING SIZE: ½ CUP

17fl oz (500ml) unsweetened almond milk

½ cup (2.8oz/80g) granular erythritol

2 egg yolks

1 tsp guar gum

1. Add the egg yolks to a heatsafe glass bowl and lightly whisk. Set aside.

2. In a medium saucepan placed over low heat, bring the almond milk and erythritol to a simmer. Continue simmering, stirring continuously, until the erythritol is dissolved.

3. Very slowly add the warm almond milk mixture to the egg yolks, a small amount at a time, while continuously whisking. Once all of the almond milk is incorporated, transfer the mixture back to the pan and place over low heat. Cook until the mixture coats the back of a spoon, then promptly remove from the heat and set aside to cool slightly.

4. Once the mixture has cooled, gradually sprinkle in the guar gum while vigorously whisking to prevent the guar gum from clumping. Continue whisking until the custard achieves a smooth, thick texture, then remove the pan from the heat.

5. Transfer the custard to small serving jars or cups. Serve warm, or allow the custard to cool completely, then cover the jars with plastic wrap and transfer to the fridge to chill for a minimum of 2 hours before serving cold. Store in the fridge for up to 3 days.

Tip If the guar gum clumps, place the mixture in a blender and blend on high for 30 seconds or until the mixture becomes creamy and frothy.

| NUTRITION PER SERVING | 50 CALORIES | 3.5g TOTAL FAT | 2g TOTAL CARBS | 1g NET CARBS | 2g PROTEIN |

NUT FREE GLUTEN FREE SUGAR FREE EGG FREE

Mascarpone Mousse with Fresh Berries

This is one of my favorite desserts! It's so easy, tastes fantastic, and relies on just a few simple ingredients. Mascarpone is an Italian soft cheese, similar to cream cheese but slightly sweeter and much creamier.

PREP TIME: **15 MINUTES**   COOK TIME: **NONE**   PASSIVE TIME: **15 MINUTES**

MAKES: 4 SERVINGS
SERVING SIZE: 1

1½ cups (8.8oz/250g) diced fresh strawberries

1 cup (8.8oz/250g) mascarpone cheese

12 drops stevia extract

½ tsp vanilla extract

1 egg, separated

1. Line the bottoms of 4 small dessert glasses with half of the diced strawberries.

2. In a medium bowl, combine the mascarpone cheese, stevia extract, vanilla extract, and egg yolk. Use a hand mixer to beat until combined.

3. In a small bowl, use a hand mixer to beat the egg white until soft peaks form. Using a spatula, gently fold the egg white into the mascarpone cheese mixture.

4. Spoon half the mixture into the dessert glasses, top with the remaining strawberries, then top with the remaining mascarpone cheese mixture.

5. Cover the glasses with plastic wrap and transfer to the fridge to chill for a minimum of 15 minutes before serving. Store in the fridge for up to 3 days.

Tip Note that there is an extremely small health risk posed by consuming raw eggs, so this recipe may not be suitable for those who are pregnant or those who may have compromised immune systems.

NUTRITION PER SERVING	300 CALORIES	30g TOTAL FAT	7.5g TOTAL CARBS	6g NET CARBS	4g PROTEIN

🌾 **GLUTEN FREE** 🍬 **SUGAR FREE**

"Rice" Pudding

Instead of rice, this recipe utilizes cauliflower as a base!
It's made deliciously thick and creamy using the same
techniques as the keto custard. It's sweet, delicious,
and rice-free! It's also a perfect breakfast treat.

PREP TIME: **10 MINUTES**	COOK TIME: **25 MINUTES**	PASSIVE TIME: **1 HOUR**

MAKES: 2 SERVINGS
SERVING SIZE: 1 CUP

1 cup (3.2oz/100g) riced
   cauliflower

1 cup (8fl oz/240ml)
   unsweetened almond milk

2 tbsp water

¼ cup granular erythritol

½ tsp ground cinnamon

¼ tsp ground nutmeg

1 tbsp butter

2 tbsp heavy whipping cream

2 large egg yolks

1. In a medium saucepan placed over medium heat, combine the riced cauliflower, almond milk, and water. Cook for 10 minutes or until the cauliflower becomes soft.

2. Add the erythritol, cinnamon, nutmeg, butter, and whipping cream. Stir until the ingredients are combined, then remove the pan from the heat. Add the egg yolks to the pan while whisking the mixture continuously to ensure the yolks don't overcook.

3. Place the pan back on the stove over low heat. Cook for 5 minutes or until the mixture thickens slightly, then remove the pan from the heat.

4. Transfer the pudding to two small serving bowls, then transfer to the fridge to chill for 1 hour. Serve chilled, or cover with plastic wrap and store in the fridge for up to 2 days.

Tip Make sure to mix the yolks very quickly once they're added to the pan to ensure they don't curdle.

NUTRITION PER SERVING	//	195 CALORIES	//	17g TOTAL FAT	//	5g TOTAL CARBS	//	3.5g NET CARBS	//	5g PROTEIN

🚫 **NUT FREE** 🌾 **GLUTEN FREE** 🚫 **SUGAR FREE**

Crème Brûlée

Traditional crème brûlée is a silky rich dessert made by baking a custard that is flavored with vanilla and topped with a layer of crunchy, caramelized sugar. This version is sugar-free, but it is every bit as decadent!

PREP TIME: **10 MINUTES**	COOK TIME: **45 MINUTES**	PASSIVE TIME: **2 HRS 30 MINS**

MAKES: 4 SERVINGS
SERVING SIZE: 1

3 large egg yolks

3 tbsp (1.2oz/40g) granular erythritol

2 cups (15.5fl oz/460ml) heavy whipping cream

1 tsp vanilla bean paste

For the topping

1 tbsp granular erythritol

1. Preheat the oven to 320°F (160°C).

2. In a medium bowl, combine the egg yolks and erythritol. Whisk until the yolks become creamy. Add the whipping cream and vanilla paste. Continue whisking until a uniform color is achieved. Transfer the mixture to 4 medium ramekins.

3. Place the ramekins on a high-sided baking sheet filled half full with water (This will help prevent the surface of the crème brûlée from cracking.) Transfer to the oven and bake for 45 minutes or until the crème brûlée is just set but still slightly wobbly in the center.

4. Very carefully remove the pan from the oven and transfer the ramekins to a cooling rack. Let cool to room temperature, then transfer the cooled ramekins to the fridge to chill for a minimum of 2 hours.

5. Prior to serving, sprinkle the remaining erythritol over the top of each ramekin and use a culinary torch to melt the erythritol to form a light crust. (Alternatively, place the ramekins under the broiler for 5 minutes.)

6. Serve promptly, or cover with plastic wrap and store in the fridge for up to two days. (If not serving right away, reserve the remaining erythritol and torch the tops only after removing the ramekins from the fridge.)

Tip Sugar alcohols don't caramelize as well as regular sugar, so this version won't have the same crunchy top layer present on traditional crème brûlée, but the erythritol will still lightly brown to create a delicate crust.

NUTRITION PER SERVING	//	447 CALORIES	//	46g TOTAL FAT	//	4g TOTAL CARBS	//	4g NET CARBS	//	5.5g PROTEIN

Ⓧ **NUT FREE** 🌾 **GLUTEN FREE** 🍬 **SUGAR FREE** Ⓞ **EGG FREE**

Chocolate Mousse

By no means is this a traditional mousse recipe, but trust me,
you'll love it! It's so deliciously fluffy and perfect for a
summer night shared with family and friends.

PREP TIME: **15 MINUTES**	COOK TIME: **NONE**	PASSIVE TIME: **30 MINUTES**

MAKES: 4 SERVINGS
SERVING SIZE: 1

1 cup (8oz/250g) full-fat cream
   cheese, warmed to room
   temperature

3 tbsp (0.9oz/25g) unsweetened
   cocoa powder

½ large ripe avocado, chopped

¼ tsp vanilla extract

3 tbsp confectioners erythritol

¼ cup (2fl oz/60ml) heavy
   whipping cream

1. Add the cream cheese to a medium bowl and use a hand mixer to beat until smooth.

2. Add the cocoa powder, avocado, vanilla extract, and erythritol. Continue beating until the ingredients are well combined, about 2 to 4 minutes.

3. In separate medium bowl, beat the heavy cream until stiff peaks form. Gently fold the whipped cream into the cream cheese mixture.

4. Spoon the mixture into small jars or cups, then transfer to the fridge to chill for a minimum of 30 minutes before serving. Cover the jars with plastic wrap and store in the fridge for up to 5 days.

Tip You can use sugar-free, pre-whipped cream just as long as it's sugar-free. Try adding a shot of espresso to enhance the flavor of the cocoa powder.

NUTRITION PER SERVING	268 CALORIES	26g TOTAL FAT	8g TOTAL CARBS	5g NET CARBS	5g PROTEIN

DAIRY FREE · GLUTEN FREE · SUGAR FREE

Chocolate Chia Seed Pudding

The chia seeds and milk in this delicious treat come together
to create a beautiful pudding-like texture that is chocolatey
and dense with a bold, nutty flavor.

PREP TIME: **20 MINUTES** COOK TIME: **NONE** PASSIVE TIME: **2 HOURS**

MAKES: 2 SERVINGS
SERVING SIZE: ½ CUP

1 cup (8fl oz/240ml) unsweetened coconut milk

3 tsp confectioners erythritol

1 tsp unsweetened cocoa powder

2 tbsp sugar-free, all-natural almond butter, divided

¼ cup (1.2oz/40g) chia seeds

2 tsp unsweetened cocoa nibs

2 tsp unsweetened coconut flakes

1. In a medium mason jar, combine the coconut milk, erythritol, cocoa powder, and 1 tablespoon of the almond butter. Tightly seal the jar and shake vigorously for 30 seconds, or until the almond butter has completely dissolved into the milk.

2. Remove the lid and add the chia seeds. Reseal the jar and shake for 1 additional minute, then transfer to the fridge to set for 5 minutes. Shake again for 1 minute. Repeat this process twice more, then leave the mixture in the fridge to set for a minimum of 2 hours or until the chia seeds become soft and the mixture thickens.

3. Divide the pudding between two serving bowls. Top with the cocoa nibs and coconut flakes, then drizzle the remaining almond butter over the top. Serve promptly, or store covered in the fridge for up to 4 days.

Tip You can substitute unsweetened almond milk or any other low-carb, unsweetened nut milk for the coconut milk.

NUTRITION PER SERVING	160 CALORIES	20g TOTAL FAT	14g TOTAL CARBS	4.5g NET CARBS	8g PROTEIN

Ⓧ **NUT FREE** Ⓖ **GLUTEN FREE** Ⓢ **SUGAR FREE**

Raspberry Soufflé

A delicate soufflé is often considered a delicacy. This keto
version is sugar-free and low-carb, and the raspberry
base gives the soufflé a wonderful pink color.

PREP TIME: **15 MINUTES**	COOK TIME: **15 MINUTES**	PASSIVE TIME: **5 MINUTES**

MAKES: 4 SERVINGS
SERVING SIZE: 1

1 tsp butter (for greasing)

1 tbsp confectioners erythritol

1 cup (4oz/120g) fresh raspberries

1 tbsp (0.5oz/15ml) water

4 large egg whites, warmed to
   room temperature

2 tbsp granular erythritol

½ tsp xanthan gum

¼ tsp salt

Zest of ½ lemon

4 tbsp clotted cream, to serve

1. Preheat the oven to 355°F (180°C). Grease 4 large ramekins with 1 teaspoon butter, then dust the insides with the confectioners erythritol.

2. Combine the raspberries and water in a food processor. Blend until smooth, then place a fine mesh sieve over a small bowl and strain the mixture. Discard the solids. Set aside.

3. Add the egg whites to a medium bowl. Using a hand mixer, beat on high until stiff peaks form.

4. Add the erythritol, xanthan gum, salt, and lemon zest to the egg whites. Mix on low until the ingredients are just combined.

5. Using a spoon, gently fold the raspberry mixture into the egg whites while being very careful not to deflate the egg whites.

6. Evenly divide the mixture between the ramekins. (If the mixture overflows the tops of the ramekins, use the backside of a knife to level off the tops.)

7. Place the ramekins on a large baking sheet. Transfer to the oven and bake for 15 minutes or until the soufflés begin to rise.

8. Top each ramekin with a dollop of the clotted cream. Serve promptly. (These desserts will not keep.)

Tip This is a tricky dessert to make, and it might take a few tries; but once you've nailed it, you will have mastered one of the most challenging recipes in this book!

NUTRITION PER SERVING	110 CALORIES	8.5g TOTAL FAT	4.5g TOTAL CARBS	2g NET CARBS	4.5g PROTEIN

🌾 GLUTEN FREE 🍬 SUGAR FREE

Fresh Berry Trifle

This decadent trifle is made with sponge cake, covered in rich cream layers and topped with low-sugar fruits. It's a colorful, festive dessert that will wow your guests!

PREP TIME: **20 MINUTES**	COOK TIME: **40 MINUTES**	PASSIVE TIME: **5 HOURS**

MAKES: 12 SERVINGS
SERVING SIZE: 5OZ (150g)

For the cake

1 cup (8.5oz/250g) full-fat ricotta cheese

⅓ cup (1.9oz/55g) granular erythritol

3 large eggs

½ cup (4oz/115g) butter, melted

¾ cup (2.5oz/70g) almond flour

1 tsp baking powder

½ tsp salt

For the filling and toppings

4 tbsp (2oz/60ml) brandy

1.2oz sugar-free, raspberry-flavored gelatin

2½ cups (19.4fl oz/575ml) hot water

3 cups (23.3fl oz/690ml) heavy whipping cream, divided

1 cup (5oz/150g) fresh raspberries (for topping)

5oz (150g) fresh strawberries, sliced (for topping)

1. Preheat the oven to 320°F (160°C), and line a 9 x 9-inch (22 x 22cm) square baking pan with parchment paper.

2. In a medium bowl, combine the ricotta cheese and erythritol, and whisk until the ingredients are combined. Continue whisking, adding 1 egg at a time, until all the eggs are incorporated into the mixture. Add the melted butter, almond flour, baking powder, and salt. Mix until well combined.

3. Pour the batter into the prepared baking pan, then transfer to the oven to bake for 40 minutes. After 30 minutes, check the cake every 5 minutes to ensure it doesn't overcook. Once a toothpick inserted into the middle comes out clean, remove the cake from the oven and set aside to cool for a minimum of 30 minutes.

4. While the cake is cooling, combine the gelatin and hot water in a small bowl. Stir continuously until the gelatin is completely dissolved. Set aside.

5. Once the cake has cooled, cut it into 2 inch (5cm) cubes. Place the cubes in a medium bowl, and pour the brandy over top. Use half the cake cubes to create a layer in the bottom of an 8 x 8-inch (20 x 20cm) trifle bowl. Cover the cubes with half of the gelatin mixture, then transfer the bowl to the fridge to chill for a minimum of 2 hours.

6. In a medium bowl, use a hand mixer to whip 2 cups of the whipping cream until soft peaks form. Spread the whipped cream evenly over the bottom layer of the trifle, then place the trifle back in the fridge to chill for an additional 30 minutes. After 30 minutes, layer the remaining cake cubes on top of the first layer, cover with remaining gelatin mixture, and place the trifle back in the fridge for an additional 2 hours.

7. Use a hand mixer to beat the remaining heavy whipping cream until stiff peaks form. Spread the whipped cream over top, then layer the raspberries and strawberry slices on top. Serve promptly, or cover and refrigerate for up to 5 days.

NUTRITION PER SERVING	390 CALORIES	37g TOTAL FAT	7.5g TOTAL CARBS	5g NET CARBS	7.5g PROTEIN

⊛ GLUTEN FREE ⊛ SUGAR FREE

"Bread" Pudding with Blueberry Compote

My mum's bread pudding was one of my favorite desserts
as a child. This version is creamy and soft, and it's just sweet
enough to satisfy a sweet tooth after a meal.

PREP TIME: **10 MINUTES**	COOK TIME: **40 MINUTES**	PASSIVE TIME: **40 MINUTES**

**MAKES: 12 SERVINGS
SERVING SIZE: 1 SLICE WITH
2 TABLESPOONS COMPOTE**

For the bread

7 large eggs

½ cup (3.5oz/100g) butter, melted

2 tbsp coconut oil, melted

1 tsp baking powder

2 cups (7oz/200g) almond flour

½ tsp salt

½ tsp xanthan gum

2 tbsp confectioners erythritol

1 tbsp unsweetened cocoa nibs

1 tsp ground cinnamon

¼ tsp ground ginger

For the pudding

3 large eggs

¾ cup (5.7fl oz/170ml)
   unsweetened almond milk

¾ cup (5.7fl oz/170ml) heavy
   whipping cream

1 tsp vanilla extract

For the compote

½ cup (5oz/150g) blueberries
   (fresh or frozen)

½ cup (4fl oz/120ml) water

1. Preheat the oven to 355°F (180°C), and line a 4.5 x 8.5-inch (11.5 x 21.5cm) loaf pan with parchment paper.

2. Combine the eggs in a large bowl and whisk for 1 minute or until the eggs become smooth and creamy. Add the butter and coconut oil, and whisk for 1 additional minute.

3. Add the baking powder, almond flour, salt, and xanthan gum. Mix until the ingredients become thick and smooth. Pour the batter into the prepared pan and transfer to the oven to bake for 45 minutes or until a toothpick inserted into the middle comes out clean. Remove from the oven to cool for 20 minutes.

4. Slice the cooled loaf into 12 equal-sized slices. Place six slices in a single layer in the bottom of a 5 x 8-inch (12 x 20cm) casserole dish, and evenly sprinkle the erythritol, cocoa nibs, cinnamon, and ginger over the slices. Repeat the process with the remaining slices.

5. Make the pudding by combining the eggs, almond milk, whipping cream, and vanilla extract in a medium bowl. Mix well to combine.

6. Pour the pudding over the bread. Transfer to the oven and bake for 30 to 40 minutes or until the egg mixture is fully cooked and set. Set aside to cool for 20 minutes.

7. While the bread pudding is baking, make the compote by combining the blueberries and water in a medium pan placed over medium heat. Bring to a boil and cook for 5 minutes, then use a potato masher to crush the ingredients until no large lumps remain.

8. Slice the cooled bread pudding into 12 equal-sized slices, then drizzle the warm compote over top of each serving. Store the bread pudding and compote in separate airtight containers for up to 7 days.

Tip The xanthan gum adds height to the bread and creates a more malleable texture, but it can be omitted if you prefer a denser bread.

NUTRITION PER SERVING	300 CALORIES	29.5g TOTAL FAT	5g TOTAL CARBS	2.5g NET CARBS	10g PROTEIN

GLUTEN FREE **SUGAR FREE** **EGG FREE**

Strawberry Cream Parfaits

European parfaits typically are made using heavy whipped cream, while Americans often make them with yogurt. This recipe is a perfect mix of the two, allowing the strawberry, hazelnut, and almond flavors to shine.

PREP TIME: **20 MINUTES**   COOK TIME: **NONE**   PASSIVE TIME: **NONE**

MAKES: 3
SERVING SIZE: 1

½ cup (4fl oz/120ml) heavy whipping cream

1⅓ cups (10fl oz/300ml) plain unsweetened Greek yogurt

1 tsp vanilla extract

4oz (150g) fresh strawberries

2 tbsp granular erythritol

¼ cup (1oz/30g) unsalted, roasted hazelnuts

¼ cup (1oz/30g) unsalted, roasted almonds

3 small sprigs fresh mint (to garnish)

1. Add the whipping cream to a medium bowl. Using a hand mixer, whip until soft peaks form, then add the Greek yogurt and vanilla extract. Gently fold until the ingredients are combined.

2. Combine the strawberries and erythritol in a high-speed blender. Blend until smooth, then transfer the mixture to a separate medium bowl. Set aside. Rinse and dry the blender container.

3. Add the hazelnuts and almonds to the blender and pulse until the nuts are finely chopped.

4. To 3 medium mason jars or dessert glasses, add equal amounts of the strawberry mixture, chopped nuts, and yogurt mixture. Top each serving with a sprig of mint. Serve promptly, or cover with plastic wrap and store in the fridge for up to 4 days.

Tip If you don't have a food processor, you can use a potato masher to mash the strawberries and a sharp knife to dice the nuts.

NUTRITION PER SERVING	363 CALORIES	33g TOTAL FAT	11g TOTAL CARBS	8.5g NET CARBS	8.5g PROTEIN

Ⓧ **NUT FREE** Ⓖ **GLUTEN FREE** Ⓢ **SUGAR FREE** Ⓔ **EGG FREE**

Chocolate Pudding

If you've been looking for the perfect chocolate dessert,
look no further! This quick and easy, no-bake pudding
is sugar-free with a decadent chocolate richness that's
smoothed out by a deliciously creamy base.

PREP TIME: **15 MINUTES**	COOK TIME: **NONE**	PASSIVE TIME: **1 HOUR**

MAKES: 4 SERVINGS
SERVING SIZE: ½ CUP
(4oz/120g)

1½ cups (12fl oz/350ml) heavy whipping cream

½ cup (2.8oz/80g) granular erythritol

½ cup (2oz/60g) unsweetened cocoa powder

½ tsp vanilla extract

¼ tsp instant coffee powder (optional)

¼ tsp xanthan gum

¼ tsp salt

1. In a small saucepan placed over low heat, combine the whipping cream, erythritol, cocoa powder, vanilla extract, salt, and instant coffee powder (if using). Simmer for 5 minutes.

2. Evenly sprinkle the xanthan gum across the surface of the heated cream mixture. Whisk vigorously until the xanthan gum is incorporated, then continue stirring until the mixture thickens.

3. Remove the pan from the heat, sprinkle in the salt, and stir.

4. Evenly divide the mixture between 4 small, sealable jars, then transfer to the fridge to chill for a minimum of 1 hour. Serve promptly, or seal the jars and store in the fridge for up to 5 days.

Tip Instant coffee powder helps enhance the flavor of the chocolate. If you prefer a more jelly-like texture, you can substitute an equal amount of unflavored gelatin for the xanthan gum.

NUTRITION PER SERVING	//	330 CALORIES	//	34g TOTAL FAT	//	8.5g TOTAL CARBS	//	4.5g NET CARBS	//	4.5g PROTEIN

🌾 **GLUTEN FREE** 🍥 **SUGAR FREE** 🍳 **EGG FREE**

Panna Cotta

Panna cotta means *cooked cream* in Italian. It's a simple dessert that takes some patience, but it's rich, silky, and full of flavor. A high-quality vanilla bean will give the best flavor, but vanilla bean paste or vanilla extract also can be used.

PREP TIME: **10 MINUTES**	COOK TIME: **20 MINUTES**	PASSIVE TIME: **12 HOURS**

MAKES: 4 SERVINGS
SERVING SIZE: 3.2OZ (100g)

1½ cups (11.5fl oz/345ml) heavy whipping cream

¼ cup (2fl oz/60ml) unsweetened almond milk

2 tbsp (.5oz/15g) granular erythritol

1 vanilla bean, halved and seeded

2 tsp powdered gelatin

¼ cup fresh raspberries (optional)

1. In a medium saucepan placed over medium heat, combine the whipping cream, almond milk, erythritol, vanilla beans, and vanilla bean pod. Bring the mixture just to a boil, then remove from the heat. Discard the vanilla bean pod.

2. While the mixture is still warm, add the gelatin and stir continuously until the gelatin is completely dissolved.

3. Divide the mixture between 2 medium ramekins. Transfer to the fridge to chill and set for a minimum of 12 hours.

4. When ready to serve, fill a flat-bottomed pan with just enough hot water to cover the sides of the ramekins (but not enough to reach the tops). Place the ramekins in the water for 1 minute, then flip them upside-down onto serving plates to remove the panna cotta from the ramekins.

5. Top each serving with the raspberries (if using) and serve promptly, or cover with plastic wrap and store in the fridge for up to 5 days.

Tip You can substitute 2 teaspoons vanilla extract or 1 teaspoon vanilla bean paste for the vanilla bean. For a raspberry compote, cook the raspberries and ¼ cup water in a saucepan, and mash the raspberries with a potato masher. Drizzle the compote over the top of the panna cotta.

NUTRITION PER SERVING (without raspberries)	631 CALORIES	65g TOTAL FAT	5.5g TOTAL CARBS	5.5g NET CARBS	7g PROTEIN

Ⓓ **DAIRY FREE** Ⓢ **NUT FREE** Ⓖ **GLUTEN FREE** Ⓢ **SUGAR FREE** Ⓔ **EGG FREE**

Blueberry Chia Pudding

I've been making this dessert for years, even before I started the ketogenic diet. The chia seeds absorb the liquid to create a deliciously soft texture, and the blueberries and coconut flakes combine to create a simple pudding that is delicious.

PREP TIME: **20 MINUTES**	COOK TIME: **NONE**	PASSIVE TIME: **2 HOURS**

MAKES: 2 SERVINGS
SERVING SIZE: ½ CUP
(5.2oz/160g)

1 cup (8fl oz/240ml) unsweetened coconut milk

1 tsp vanilla extract

3 tsp confectioners erythritol

¼ cup (1.2oz/40g) chia seeds

¼ cup fresh blueberries

2 tbsp unsweetened coconut flakes

1. In a medium mason jar, combine the coconut milk, vanilla extract, and erythritol. Tightly seal the jar and shake vigorously for 30 seconds.

2. Remove the lid and add the chia seeds. Reseal the jar and shake for 1 additional minute. Transfer the jar to the fridge for 5 minutes, then shake again for 1 minute. Repeat this process two more times, then leave the mixture in the refrigerator for 2 hours or until the chia seeds become soft and the mixture thickens.

3. To serve, divide the pudding between two serving bowls or dessert jars, and top with the blueberries and coconut flakes, or tightly seal the mason jar and store in the fridge for up to 5 days.

Tip Unsweetened almond milk or any other low-carb, unsweetened nut milk can be substituted for the coconut milk.

NUTRITION PER SERVING	//	160 CALORIES	//	12g TOTAL FAT	//	11g TOTAL CARBS	//	3.5g NET CARBS	//	4g PROTEIN

🍦 **DAIRY FREE** 🚫 **NUT FREE** 🌾 **GLUTEN FREE** 🚫 **SUGAR FREE**

Coconut Custard

This baked custard is a spin on a Thai dessert, which traditionally is made with coconut cream, eggs, and pandan leaves. Because pandan leaves may be difficult to get, this recipe uses vanilla extract to achieve a similar flavor.

PREP TIME: **5 MINUTES**	COOK TIME: **20 MINUTES**	PASSIVE TIME: **30 MINUTES**

MAKES: 2 SERVINGS
SERVING SIZE: 1

¾ cup (5.5fl oz/160ml) unsweetened canned coconut cream

4 eggs

30 drops stevia extract

1 tsp vanilla extract

1. Place a steamer tray in a large pot and add 3 cups water. Bring the water to a boil over high heat.

2. In a medium mixing bowl, combine the coconut cream, eggs, stevia extract, and vanilla extract. Whisk to combine, then divide the mixture between 2 large ramekins.

3. Using tongs, carefully place the ramekins on the steamer rack. Cover the pot and steam for 20 minutes.

4. Using tongs, carefully transfer the ramekins to a cooling rack and let cool for a minimum of 15 minutes, then transfer to the fridge to chill for an additional 15 minutes prior to serving. Cover with plastic wrap and store in the fridge for up to 5 days.

Tip You also can top this custard with fresh berries or a sprinkle of cinnamon. For a more authentic flavor, substitute an equal amount of pandan leaf extract for the vanilla extract.

NUTRITION PER SERVING	422 CALORIES	38g TOTAL FAT	6.5g TOTAL CARBS	5g NET CARBS	15g PROTEIN

🌾 **GLUTEN FREE** 🍬 **SUGAR FREE**

Sticky Toffee Pudding

Sticky date pudding was a favorite dessert of mine as a child, but since dates are high in carbs, I had to create a low-carb substitute. This sticky toffee treat does the trick, and is one of my favorite recipes in the book.

PREP TIME: **10 MINUTES**	COOK TIME: **30 MINUTES**	PASSIVE TIME: **15 MINUTES**

MAKES: 8 SERVINGS
SERVING SIZE: 1 SLICE AND 3 TBSP CARAMEL SAUCE

1 cup (3.5oz/100g) almond flour

⅓ cup (1.2oz/40g) coconut flour

½ cup (2.8oz/80g) granular erythritol

½ tsp baking powder

⅓ cup (2.6oz/75g) butter, melted

2 large eggs, warmed to room temperature

2 tsp vanilla extract

Caramel Sauce (see p. 133), warmed

1. Preheat the oven to 355°F (180°C), and line a 5 x 9-inch (13 x 23cm) loaf pan with parchment paper.

2. In a medium bowl, combine the almond flour, coconut flour, erythritol, and baking powder. Mix until well combined, then add the melted butter, eggs, and vanilla extract. Stir to combine.

3. Pour the mixture into the prepared pan and transfer to the oven to bake for 30 minutes or until a toothpick inserted into the center comes out clean. Set aside to cool slightly for 15 minutes.

4. Using a knife, poke holes in the pudding in 1-inch (2.5cm) increments to allow the caramel sauce to penetrate the pudding. Cut the pudding into 8 equal-sized portions.

5. Place each slice on a serving plate and drizzle 3 tablespoons of the warm caramel sauce over top of each serving. Serve promptly, or store the pudding and caramel sauce in separate airtight containers in the fridge for up to 1 week. (Reheat prior to serving.)

Tip It's best to add the sauce after you have plated the pudding to help minimize mess and also to control the portion size.

NUTRITION PER SERVING	335 CALORIES	33g TOTAL FAT	6g TOTAL CARBS	6g NET CARBS	5.5g PROTEIN

⚜ **GLUTEN FREE** ⚜ **SUGAR FREE**

Chocolate-dipped Éclairs

The éclair is a classic French dessert, and this low-carb
version is easier to make than you might think!

PREP TIME: **20 MINUTES**	COOK TIME: **40 MINUTES**	PASSIVE TIME: **1 HOUR**

MAKES: 12
SERVING SIZE: 1

For the pastry fingers

1 tbsp heavy whipping cream
¾ cup (6fl oz/180ml) water
¼ cup (2oz/60g) unsalted butter
6 drops stevia extract
¼ tsp salt
½ tsp xanthan gum
½ cup (1.4oz/50g) almond flour
1 tbsp psyllium husk powder
2 large eggs, warmed to room
   temperature

For the custard filling

¾ cup (8.5fl oz/250ml)
   unsweetened almond milk
½ cup (4fl oz/120ml) heavy
   whipping cream
½ cup granular erythritol
2 tsp vanilla extract
1 tsp powdered gelatin
1 tbsp butter

For the chocolate ganache

⅓ cup (2.8fl oz/80ml) heavy
   whipping cream
1.8oz (50g) unsweetened dark
   baking chocolate, diced
⅓ cup confectioners erythritol

1. Preheat the oven to 390°F (200°C), and line a large baking tray with
   parchment paper.

2. Make the pastry fingers by combining the whipping cream, water, and
   butter in a medium saucepan placed over medium heat. Once the butter is
   melted, add the stevia, salt, and xanthan gum. Stir well. Add the almond
   flour and psyllium husk powder, and stir until the mixture becomes thick.
   Transfer to a large bowl. Using a hand mixer, blend the mixture on low,
   allowing the mixture cool slightly, then add the eggs, one at a time, while
   continuously mixing on low.

3. Transfer the mixture to a large piping bag fitted with a ¾-inch (2cm) star
   nozzle. On the prepared baking tray, pipe the mixture out into 12 tube-
   shaped pastries that are approximately 6 x 1.5 inches (15 x 3.75cm each).
   Transfer to the oven, bake for 10 minutes, then reduce the temperature
   to 320°F (160°C) and bake for an additional 30 minutes or until the pastries
   turn golden brown.

4. While the pastries are baking, make the custard filling by combining the
   almond milk, whipping cream, erythritol, vanilla extract, gelatin, and butter
   in a medium saucepan placed over medium heat. Whisk continuously until
   the mixture becomes slightly thick. Transfer the mixture to a medium bowl,
   cover with plastic wrap, and place in the fridge to cool for 1 hour, stirring the
   mixture every 20 minutes.

5. Cut the ends from each pastry, then use a knife to bore a small void through
   the middle of each pastry. Transfer the cooled filling to a piping bag and fill
   each pastry with the custard. Place the pastries on a serving plate. Set aside.

6. Make the ganache by microwaving the whipping cream on high for 1
   minute, then add the chocolate. Let the mixture sit for 2 minutes, then add the
   erythritol and stir until a smooth, creamy texture is achieved. Transfer to a
   shallow plate.

7. Dip the tops of the éclairs in the ganache and place them, dipped-sides-up,
   on the serving plate. Transfer to the fridge to chill for a minimum of 1 hour.
   Store in an airtight container in the fridge for up to 4 days.

NUTRITION PER SERVING	170 CALORIES	16.5g TOTAL FAT	3.5g TOTAL CARBS	2g NET CARBS	4g PROTEIN

CHAPTER 4

Cookies, Blondies, and Brownies

Who would have ever believed that you could enjoy soft, chewy cookies on keto? With these recipes, you'll do just that, and also enjoy brownies, biscotti, and more.

🌾 **GLUTEN FREE** 🍬 **SUGAR FREE**

Chocolate Chip Cookies

This is possibly one of the best recipes I've ever created! These cookies are soft and chewy, and they're virtually indistinguishable from the real thing. If there's only one recipe you make from this book, make this one!

PREP TIME: **10 MINUTES**	COOK TIME: **10 MINUTES**	PASSIVE TIME: **30 MINUTES**

MAKES: 12
SERVING SIZE: 1

½ cup (3.5oz/100g) unsalted butter, melted

1 cup (4.5oz/130g) granular erythritol

1 tsp vanilla extract

1 large egg

2 cups (6oz/170g) almond meal

½ tsp xanthan gum

½ tsp baking powder

¼ tsp salt

½ cup (3oz/90g) unsweetened chocolate chips

1. Preheat the oven to 355°F (180°C).

2. In a medium bowl, combine the butter and erythritol. Using a hand mixer, beat the ingredients on medium for 1 minute, then add the vanilla extract and egg and mix on low for an additional 20 seconds.

3. Add the almond meal, xanthan gum, baking powder, and salt. Mix until well combined, then fold in the chocolate chips.

4. Remove the dough from the bowl (you should be able to pick it up with your hands) and divide it into 12 equal-sized pieces. Roll the pieces into balls and evenly space them across a large baking sheet. Transfer to the oven and bake for 10 minutes.

5. Remove the cookies from the oven and let them cool for a minimum of 30 minutes before serving. Store in an airtight container in the fridge for up to 1 week.

Tip If you don't have almond meal, almond flour also will work, but don't use a super-fine ground variety, as the dough will not spread out in the oven.

NUTRITION PER SERVING	//	168 CALORIES	//	17g TOTAL FAT	//	2.3g TOTAL CARBS	//	1.4g NET CARBS	//	3.5g PROTEIN

🌾 **GLUTEN FREE** 🍬 **SUGAR FREE**

Peanut Butter Cookies

These cookies are delicious and a perfect on-the-go snack.
This simple recipe is quick to prepare, so you can make a
batch anytime you get a craving for something sweet!

PREP TIME: **15 MINUTES**	COOK TIME: **15 MINUTES**	PASSIVE TIME: **30 MINUTES**

MAKES: 12
SERVING SIZE: 1

¾ cup (7oz/200g) all-natural, sugar-free crunchy peanut butter

¼ cup (1.4oz/40g) granular erythritol

1 large egg

½ tsp vanilla extract

¼ tsp salt

¼ cup (1.9oz/55g) unsalted butter, melted

1. Preheat the oven to 355°F (180°C).

2. Combine all of the ingredients in a medium bowl. Mix until the ingredients are well combined and a uniform color is achieved.

3. Using a tablespoon measuring spoon, measure out 12 portions onto a large baking tray. Use a fork to press the cookies down flat, making sure to press horizontally and vertically to create uniform shapes.

4. Bake for 15 minutes or until the cookies turn golden brown. Transfer to a cooling rack and let them cool to room temperature. Store in an airtight container in the fridge for up to 1 week.

Tip For almond butter cookies, substitute an equal amount of all-natural, sugar-free almond butter for the peanut butter.

NUTRITION PER SERVING	140 CALORIES	12.5g TOTAL FAT	3.5g TOTAL CARBS	2g NET CARBS	4.5g PROTEIN

🌾 **GLUTEN FREE** 🍬 **SUGAR FREE**

Gingerbread Cookies

These traditional holiday cookies have a crisp outer layer
that's surrounded by a soft chewy center and feature
warm notes of ginger, cinnamon, and cloves.

| PREP TIME: **20 MINUTES** | COOK TIME: **12 MINUTES** | PASSIVE TIME: **1 HOUR** |

MAKES: 18
SERVING SIZE: 1

½ cup (3.2oz/100g) unsalted
  butter, melted

½ cup (2.8oz/80g) granular
  erythritol

1 large egg

2½ tbsp coconut flour

1 cup (3.2oz/100g) almond flour

1 tbsp baking powder

½ tsp xanthan gum

¼ tsp ground cloves

¼ tsp allspice

1 tsp ground ginger

½ tsp ground cinnamon

¼ tsp ground nutmeg

1 egg yolk

1. In a medium bowl, combine the melted butter, erythritol, and egg. Whisk until the ingredients are well combined.

2. In a separate medium bowl, combine the coconut flour, almond flour, baking powder, xanthan gum, cloves, allspice, ginger, cinnamon, and nutmeg. Mix until the ingredients are well combined and a uniform color is achieved. Add the egg yolk and gently stir to combine.

3. Add the butter mixture to the dry ingredients, and use a rubber spatula to mix the ingredients until they're well combined. (The mixture may look wet, which is fine.)

4. Pour the dough out onto a large sheet of plastic wrap. Tightly pull the edges of the plastic wrap together to pull the dough up into a ball, then tie the ends to hold the dough in place. Transfer to the fridge for 1 hour to chill and also to help the coconut flour absorb the liquid.

5. Preheat the oven to 335°F (170°C), and line a large baking sheet with parchment paper.

6. Divide the chilled dough into 18 equal-sized balls and place them on the baking sheet. Use the bottom of a drinking glass to press the cookies flat to about a ¼-inch (5mm) thickness.

7. Transfer to the oven and bake for 12 minutes or until the cookies turn a golden brown. Store at room temperature in an airtight container for up to 1 week.

Tip If you have a gingerbread man cookie cutter, you can roll out the dough flat and use the cutter to create gingerbread man cookies.

| NUTRITION PER SERVING | 83 CALORIES | 8g TOTAL FAT | 1.5g TOTAL CARBS | 0.9g NET CARBS | 1.8g PROTEIN |

GLUTEN FREE SUGAR FREE

Salted Caramel Blondies

Unlike brownies, which feature cocoa and chocolate flavors,
blondies feature brown sugar and caramel flavors. This recipe
captures those flavors but uses butter, sugar, and
alcohol sweeteners instead of sugar.

PREP TIME: **15 MINUTES**	COOK TIME: **40 MINUTES**	PASSIVE TIME: **2 HRS 15 MIN**

MAKES: 16
SERVING SIZE: 1

For the blondies

1 cup (7oz/200g) unsalted butter

1 cup (6oz/180g) granular erythritol

⅔ cup (2oz/60g) almond flour

2 tbsp coconut flour

½ tsp guar gum

½ tsp salt

1 tsp baking powder

3 large eggs

1 tsp vanilla extract

For the salted caramel topping

½ cup (3.5oz/100g) unsalted butter

½ cup (3.5fl oz/125ml) heavy whipping cream

½ cup (3oz/90g) granular erythritol

½ tsp vanilla extract

1 tsp salt

¼ tsp citric acid powder

1. Preheat the oven to 355°F (180°C), and line an 8 x 8-inch (20 x 20cm) square baking pan with parchment paper.

2. Make the batter for the blondies by placing the butter in a medium saucepan placed over medium heat. Heat the butter, stirring continuously, until it browns, but doesn't burn, then add the erythritol and promptly remove the pan from the heat. Stir and set aside to cool.

3. In a medium bowl, sift the almond flour, coconut flour, guar gum, salt, and baking powder. Mix until a uniform color is achieved.

4. In a separate medium bowl, combine the eggs and vanilla extract. Whisk vigorously, then slowly add the almond flour mixture, and stir until well combined. Slowly add the melted butter mixture. Pour the mixture into the prepared pan, and transfer to the oven to bake for 30 minutes. Remove from the oven and set aside to cool for 15 minutes.

5. Make the salted caramel topping by adding the butter to a medium saucepan placed over medium heat. Heat the butter until it browns but doesn't burn.

6. Add the heavy cream and erythritol. Continue stirring until the mixture comes to a boil, then add the vanilla extract, salt, and citric acid powder. Stir, then remove the pan from the heat and allow the mixture to cool to room temperature, about 15 minutes. Once the topping mixture has cooled, use an immersion blender to blend until smooth.

7. Pour the cooled topping over the blondies to create a top caramel layer. Transfer to the fridge to set and cool for a minimum of 2 hours. Serve chilled, or store in an airtight container in the fridge for up to 7 days.

Tip Be extra careful not to let the butter burn. It can change the flavor of the recipe.

NUTRITION PER SERVING	// 214 CALORIES	// 22.5g TOTAL FAT	// 1g TOTAL CARBS	// 0.5g NET CARBS	// 2.5g PROTEIN

🌾 **GLUTEN FREE** 🍬 **SUGAR FREE**

Biscotti

Biscotti translates to "cookie" in Italian. This recipe combines
the sweetness of ground cardamom with aromatic orange
zest and vanilla to create a beautifully crunchy texture that
can be dipped in coffee or enjoyed on its own.

PREP TIME: **15 MINUTES**	COOK TIME: **40 MINUTES**	PASSIVE TIME: **30 MINUTES**

MAKES: 24
SERVING SIZE: 1

1 cup (5oz/140g) whole raw almonds

¼ cup (2oz/60g) butter, warmed to room temperature

½ cup (2.8oz/80g) granular erythritol

2 large eggs

¼ tsp ground cardamom

1 tbsp orange zest

1 tsp vanilla extract

1½ cups (5oz/150g) almond flour

¼ cup (1oz/30g) coconut flour

1 tsp xanthan gum

1. Preheat the oven to 355°F (180°C), and line a large baking sheet with parchment paper.

2. Spread the almonds in a single layer across a second large baking sheet. Transfer to the oven, toast for 10 minutes, then transfer to a cutting board and roughly chop. Set aside to cool for 10 minutes.

3. In a medium bowl, combine the butter and erythritol. Using a hand mixer, mix until the ingredients are combined, then add the eggs, cardamom, orange zest, and vanilla extract. Continue to mix until well combined.

4. In a separate bowl, combine the almond flour, coconut flour, and xanthan gum. Stir until a uniform color is achieved.

5. Add the dry ingredients to the wet ingredients and stir to combine. Stir in the chopped almonds once the mixture begins to thicken.

6. Divide the mixture into two equal portions, then shape them into elongated rolls that are similar to large baguettes and about 7 inches (17cm) long and 2 inches (5cm) wide. Transfer both pieces to the prepared baking sheet and place in the oven to bake for 25 minutes.

7. Remove the rolls from the oven and while they're still hot, cut them into 12 equal slices at 45-degree angles.

8. Return the slices to the baking sheet with the cut sides facing up. Place them back in the oven and bake for an additional 15 minutes, flipping the slices halfway through the baking time.

9. Remove the biscotti from the oven and allow to cool completely before serving. Store in an airtight container in the fridge for up to 1 week.

Tip Cutting the biscotti rolls while they're still hot helps prevent the edges from crumbling and also makes the almonds easier to slice.

NUTRITION PER SERVING	100 CALORIES	9g TOTAL FAT	3g TOTAL CARBS	1.5g NET CARBS	3g PROTEIN

🌾 **GLUTEN FREE** 🍯 **SUGAR FREE**

Salted Caramel Brownies

Zesty salted caramel and creamy chocolate brownies
is a scrumptious flavor pairing. If you love brownies,
this buttery beast will be a delicious treat!

PREP TIME: **15 MINUTES**	COOK TIME: **40 MINUTES**	PASSIVE TIME: **2 HRS 15 MIN**

MAKES: 16
SERVING SIZE: 1

For the brownies

⅔ cup (2oz/60g) almond flour

¼ cup (1oz/30g) Dutch cocoa powder

1 tsp baking powder

½ tsp guar gum

1 tsp instant espresso powder

½ tsp salt

½ cup (3.2oz/100g) unsweetened baking chocolate, chopped

½ cup (3.5oz/100g) unsalted butter

3 large eggs

1 cup (6oz/180g) granular erythritol

1 tsp vanilla extract

½ tsp sea salt flakes

For the salted caramel topping

½ cup (3.5oz/100g) unsalted butter

½ cup (3.5fl oz/125ml) heavy whipping cream

½ cup (3oz/90g) granular erythritol

½ tsp vanilla extract

1 tsp salt

¼ tsp citric acid powder

1. Preheat the oven to 355°F (180°C), and line an 8 x 8-inch (20 x 20cm) square baking pan with parchment paper.

2. In a medium bowl, sift together the almond flour, cocoa powder, baking powder, guar gum, espresso powder, and salt. Mix until a uniform color is achieved. Set aside.

3. Add the chopped chocolate to a small bowl. Melt the butter in a small saucepan placed over low heat, then pour the melted butter over top of the chocolate. Let the mixture sit for 5 minutes, then stir to combine. Set aside.

4. In a separate medium bowl, combine the eggs and erythritol. Whisk vigorously while slowly adding the almond flour mixture. Continue whisking until the ingredients are well combined, add the melted chocolate mixture, and stir to combine.

5. Transfer the mixture to the prepared baking pan. Bake for 20 minutes, remove the pan from the oven, and drop it hard on a flat surface to level out the brownies. Sprinkle the sea salt flakes over the top and return the brownies to the oven to bake for an additional 10 minutes.

6. While the brownies are baking, make the salted caramel topping by adding the butter to a medium saucepan placed over medium heat. Heat the butter until it browns but does not burn, then add the whipping cream and erythritol. Continue stirring until the mixture comes to a boil, then add the vanilla extract, salt, and citric acid. Stir and remove the pan from the heat. Allow the mixture to cool to room temperature, about 15 minutes, then use an immersion blender to blend until smooth.

7. Pour the salted caramel sauce over the brownies, cover, and transfer to the fridge to set for a minimum of 2 hours. Store in an airtight container in the fridge for up to 1 week.

NUTRITION PER SERVING	//	202 CALORIES	//	20g TOTAL FAT	//	4g TOTAL CARBS	//	2.5g NET CARBS	//	3.5g PROTEIN

🌾 **GLUTEN FREE** 🍬 **SUGAR FREE** 🥚 **EGG FREE**

Shortbread Cookies

This keto version of a classic cookie is made with some not-so-classic ingredients, but it tastes just like the original! These cookies pair wonderfully with tea or coffee.

PREP TIME: **10 MINUTES**	COOK TIME: **15 MINUTES**	PASSIVE TIME: **30 MINUTES**

MAKES: 12
SERVING SIZE: 1

1 cup (8oz/230g) unsalted butter, melted

½ cup (2.8oz/80g) granular erythritol

5 drops stevia extract

1 tsp vanilla extract

1 tsp lemon zest

1 cup (3.5oz/100g) almond flour

½ cup (1.2oz/40g) coconut flour

½ tsp xanthan gum

1 tsp baking powder

½ tsp salt

1. Preheat the oven to 355°F (180°C), and line a large baking sheet with parchment paper.

2. In a large bowl, combine the melted butter and erythritol. Using a hand mixer, beat the ingredients for 1 minute, then add the stevia extract, vanilla extract, and lemon zest, and mix on low for 20 additional seconds. Set aside.

3. In a separate large bowl, combine the almond flour, coconut flour, xanthan gum, baking powder, and salt. Mix until well combined.

4. Add the wet ingredients to the dry ingredients. Use a hand mixer to mix until well combined.

5. Using a small ice cream scoop or a tablespoon, spoon out tablespoon-sized portions of the dough onto the prepared baking sheet. Using a fork, press the cookies down flat in both directions, and smooth out any cracked edges. Transfer to the oven to bake for 15 minutes or until the cookies begin to brown on the edges.

6. Remove the cookies from the oven and transfer to a cooling rack to cool to room temperature. Store in an airtight container in the fridge for up to 1 week.

Tip In a pinch, guar gum is a suitable substitute for the xanthan gum; however, gelatin won't work because it doesn't set hard, which means the cookies will not be firm.

NUTRITION PER SERVING	200 CALORIES	20g TOTAL FAT	3.5g TOTAL CARBS	1.5g NET CARBS	2.5g PROTEIN

GLUTEN FREE · SUGAR FREE

Snickerdoodles

These sugar-free cookies are incredibly soft and airy,
and they're absolutely delicious. The flavor is similar to
cinnamon French toast covered in maple syrup!

PREP TIME: **10 MINUTES**	COOK TIME: **10 MINUTES**	PASSIVE TIME: **30 MINUTES**

MAKES: 12
SERVING SIZE: 2

½ cup (3.5oz/100g) unsalted butter, melted

¼ cup (2oz/60g) granular erythritol

1 tsp vanilla extract

⅓ cup (2fl oz/60ml) maple-flavored sugar-free syrup

2 tsp ground cinnamon

1 large egg

2 cups (6oz/170g) almond meal

½ tsp xanthan gum

½ tsp baking powder

¼ tsp salt

For dusting

2 tsp confectioners erythritol

2 tsp ground cinnamon

1. Preheat the oven to 355°F (180°C).

2. Combine the melted butter and erythritol in a medium bowl. Using a hand mixer, beat the ingredients on medium for 1 minute, then add the vanilla extract, maple-flavored syrup, cinnamon, and egg. Mix on low for an additional 20 seconds.

3. Add the almond meal, xanthan gum, baking powder, and salt. Mix until well combined, then transfer the mixture to the fridge to allow the ingredients to set for 20 minutes.

4. Roll out the chilled dough into a log shape and divide it into 12 equal-sized pieces. Roll the pieces into balls.

5. Combine the cinnamon and erythritol on a small plate. Roll the balls in the mixture until they're coated, then transfer the balls to a large baking sheet.

6. Using a fork, press down on the balls in both directions until they're almost flat, but leave enough height that the cookies will still spread as they bake.

7. Bake for 10 minutes, then transfer to a cooling rack. Store in an airtight container in the fridge for up to 1 week.

Tip If you prefer not to use the maple-flavored syrup, omit the syrup and increase the total erythritol to 1 cup.

NUTRITION PER SERVING	320 CALORIES	30g TOTAL FAT	5g TOTAL CARBS	2.8g NET CARBS	7g PROTEIN

🌾 GLUTEN FREE 🍬 SUGAR FREE

Chocolate Brownies

You simply can't walk past a good fudgy chocolate brownie.
The espresso powder and salt enhance the chocolate flavor
and give these brownies a unique edge.

PREP TIME: **15 MINUTES**	COOK TIME: **40 MINUTES**	PASSIVE TIME: **30 MINUTES**

MAKES: 16
SERVING SIZE: 1

⅔ cup (2oz/60g) almond flour

¼ cup (1oz/30g) Dutch cocoa powder

1 tsp baking powder

½ tsp guar gum

1 tsp espresso powder

½ tsp salt

½ cup (3.2oz/100g) unsweetened baking chocolate, chopped

½ cup (3.5oz/100g) unsalted butter

3 large eggs

1 cup (6oz/180g) granular erythritol

1 tsp vanilla extract

½ tsp sea salt flakes

1. Preheat the oven to 355°F (180°C), and line an 8 x 8-inch (20 x 20cm) brownie pan with parchment paper.

2. In a medium bowl, sift together the almond flour, cocoa powder, baking powder, guar gum, espresso powder, and salt. Stir until a uniform color is achieved. Set aside.

3. Add the chopped chocolate to a small bowl. Melt the butter in a small saucepan placed over low heat, then pour the melted butter over the top of the chocolate. Let the ingredients sit for 5 minutes, then stir to combine.

4. In large bowl, combine the eggs, erythritol, and vanilla extract, and whisk until the ingredients are combined. Slowly add the dry ingredients, while continuously whisking, until all the ingredients are well combined

5. Add the melted chocolate and butter mixture, and stir to combine. Pour the batter into the prepared brownie pan. Transfer to the oven and bake for 20 minutes.

6. After 20 minutes, remove the pan from the oven, drop it hard on a flat surface to level out the brownies, then sprinkle the salt flakes over the top. Return the brownies to the oven to bake for an additional 10 minutes.

7. After 10 minutes, insert a toothpick into the center of the brownies. If the toothpick comes out clean, remove the brownies from the oven and set aside to cool for 20 minutes before slicing. Store in an airtight container in the fridge for up to 1 week.

Tip If you don't have espresso powder, you can use freeze-dried instant coffee or add a shot of espresso to the batter. If you don't have Dutch cocoa powder, you can use regular cocoa powder, but the brownies won't be as dense.

NUTRITION PER SERVING	//	126 CALORIES	//	11.5g TOTAL FAT	//	3g TOTAL CARBS	//	1g NET CARBS	//	3g PROTEIN

GLUTEN FREE **SUGAR FREE**

Lemon "Sugar" Cookies

If you love lemon and you love a buttery sugar cookie,
you'll fall in love with this recipe! The combination of
the zest of lemon and a buttery finish will convince
any sugar addict that these are the real deal.

PREP TIME: **10 MINUTES**	COOK TIME: **20 MINUTES**	PASSIVE TIME: **20 MINUTES**

MAKES: 12
SERVING SIZE: 1

1½ cups (4.5oz/135g) almond flour

⅓ cup (1oz/30g) coconut flour

½ tsp baking powder

¼ tsp salt

½ tsp xanthan gum

1 cup (8oz/230g) unsalted butter,
   warmed to room temperature

½ cup (2oz/60g) granular
   erythritol

10 drops stevia extract

1 tsp vanilla extract

1 large egg

Juice of 2 medium lemons
   (about 1.2fl oz/40ml)

1. Preheat the oven to 355°F (180°C) and line a large baking sheet with parchment paper.

2. In a medium bowl, combine the almond flour, coconut flour, baking powder, salt, and xanthan gum. Mix until a uniform color is achieved.

3. In a second medium bowl, combine the butter, erythritol, stevia extract, vanilla extract, egg, and lemon juice. Using a hand mixer, mix until the ingredients are well combined.

4. Slowly add the almond flour mixture to the butter mixture. Continue mixing until the ingredients are well combined.

5. Using a medium-sized ice cream scoop or a large spoon, scoop out 12 equal-sized portions of the dough. Roll each portion into a ball and place them on the prepared baking sheet. Using a fork, press down on the cookies in both directions until they're flat.

6. Transfer the cookies to the oven and bake for 20 minutes or until they turn golden brown on the edges. Let the cookies cool completely before serving. Store in an airtight container in the fridge for up to 1 week.

Tip These cookies will be very soft when they come out of the oven, so it's important to let them cool completely prior to serving or storing.

NUTRITION PER SERVING	225 CALORIES	22g TOTAL FAT	4g TOTAL CARBS	2g NET CARBS	3.5g PROTEIN

GLUTEN FREE **SUGAR FREE**

Cream Cheese Cookies

These soft and delightfully chewy cookies will impress anyone
with a sweet tooth, even if they don't eat keto! They have
a light and airy texture, they're sugar- and gluten-free,
and they're incredibly simple to make.

PREP TIME: **10 MINUTES**	COOK TIME: **20 MINUTES**	PASSIVE TIME: **20 MINUTES**

MAKES: 12
SERVING SIZE: 1

2 cups (6oz/170g) almond flour

½ tsp baking powder

¼ tsp salt

½ tsp xanthan gum

½ cup (3.5oz/100g) full-fat cream
cheese, warmed to room
temperature

½ cup (3.5oz/100g) unsalted
butter, warmed to room
temperature

½ cup (2oz/60g) granular
erythritol

10 drops stevia extract

1 tsp vanilla extract

1 large egg

1. Preheat the oven to 355°F (180°C), and line a large baking sheet with
   parchment paper.

2. In a medium bowl, combine the almond flour, baking powder, salt, and
   xanthan gum. Stir until a uniform color is achieved.

3. In a separate medium bowl, combine the cream cheese and butter. Using a
   hand mixer, mix until the ingredients are combined, then add the erythritol,
   stevia extract, vanilla extract, and egg. Mix until the ingredients are well
   combined.

4. Slowly add the almond flour mixture to the butter mixture. Continue mixing
   until the ingredients are combined.

5. Using a medium-sized ice cream scoop or a large spoon, scoop out 12 equal-
   sized portions of the dough. Roll each portion into a ball and place them on
   the prepared baking sheet. Using a fork, press down on the cookies in both
   directions until they're flat.

6. Transfer the cookies to the oven and bake for 20 minutes or until they turn
   golden brown on the edges. Let the cookies cool completely before serving.
   Store in an airtight container in the fridge for up to 1 week.

Tip These cookies will be very soft when they come out of the oven, so it's important to let
them cool completely before serving or storing.

NUTRITION PER SERVING	180 CALORIES	17g TOTAL FAT	3.5g TOTAL CARBS	1.5g NET CARBS	4g PROTEIN

🌾 **GLUTEN FREE** 🍭 **SUGAR FREE**

Coconut Cookies

Coconut cookies were an all-time favorite for me as a kid.
These cookies are completely sugar- and gluten-free,
and they're delicious paired with coffee or tea!

PREP TIME: **10 MINUTES**	COOK TIME: **20 MINUTES**	PASSIVE TIME: **20 MINUTES**

MAKES: 8
SERVING SIZE: 1

1 cup (8oz/230g) unsalted butter

½ cup (2.8oz/80g) granular erythritol

2 drops stevia extract

1 cup (3oz/90g) almond flour

1 cup (3.5oz/100g) unsweetened desiccated coconut

⅓ cup (1oz/30g) unsweetened shredded coconut

½ tsp baking powder

¼ tsp salt

½ tsp xanthan gum

1 tsp vanilla extract

1 large egg

1. Preheat the oven to 355°F (180°C), and line a large baking sheet with parchment paper.

2. Add the butter to a medium saucepan placed over medium heat. Stirring continuously, heat the butter until it browns but doesn't burn, then add the erythritol and stevia. Stir and promptly remove the pan from the heat. Set aside to cool.

3. In a medium bowl, combine the almond flour, desiccated coconut, shredded coconut, baking powder, salt, and xanthan gum. Stir until a uniform color is achieved.

4. Pour the butter mixture into the almond flour mixture, and add the vanilla extract. Mix well, then add the egg. Mix until well combined.

5. Using a medium-sized ice cream scoop or large spoon, scoop out 8 equal-sized portions of the dough. Roll each portion into balls and place them on the prepared baking sheet.

6. Using a fork, flatten the balls by pressing down on the cookies in both directions. Transfer to the fridge to chill and set for 20 minutes.

7. After 20 minutes, remove the cookies from the fridge and transfer to the oven to bake for 20 minutes or until they turn golden brown on the edges. Let the cookies cool to room temperature before serving. Store in an airtight container in the fridge for up to 1 week.

Tip These cookies will be very soft when they come out of the oven, so it's important to let them cool completely before serving or storing.

NUTRITION PER SERVING	270 CALORIES	26.5g TOTAL FAT	7g TOTAL CARBS	5g NET CARBS	2.5g PROTEIN

CHAPTER 5

Bars, Pies, and Tarts

Satisfying bars loaded with nuts, fruit, and coconut, warm and decadent fruit and meringue pies, and gooey iced cinnamon rolls are all featured in this chapter.

🐄 **DAIRY FREE** 🌾 **GLUTEN FREE** 🍯 **SUGAR FREE** 🥚 **EGG FREE**

Strawberry Cashew Bars

These delicious bars are dairy-free and simple to make.
They're the perfect treat to enjoy with a glass of
dry champagne on a hot summer afternoon.

PREP TIME: **40 MINUTES**	COOK TIME: **NONE**	PASSIVE TIME: **7 HOURS**

MAKES: 18
SERVING SIZE: 1

For the base

1½ cups (5oz/150g) raw almonds

¾ cup (3oz/90g) raw walnuts

½ tsp sea salt

10 drops stevia extract

For the filling

2 cups (7oz/200g) raw, unsalted
cashews

13.5fl oz (400ml) can
unsweetened coconut cream

2 tbsp coconut oil

Juice of ½ lemon

1 tsp vanilla extract

30 drops stevia extract

9oz (250g) fresh strawberries,
divided

2 tsp powdered gelatin

1. Place the cashews in a large bowl and cover with water. Set aside to soak for a minimum of 4 hours.

2. Make the base by combining the almonds, walnuts, sea salt, and stevia extract in a food processor. Pulse just until a semi-fine texture is achieved.

3. Line an 11 x 7-inch (28 x 18cm) baking pan with parchment paper. Press the base mixture flat into the bottom of the pan. Transfer to the fridge to set for 30 minutes.

4. While the base is setting, make the filling by combining the soaked cashews, coconut cream, coconut oil, lemon juice, vanilla extract, stevia extract, and half of the strawberries in a food processor. Begin processing while slowly adding the gelatin to the mixture. Process until a smooth consistency is achieved and no lumps remain.

5. Evenly spread the filling over the base. Return the pan to the fridge to allow the bars to set for 30 additional minutes. While the bars are setting, thinly slice the remaining strawberries.

6. Once the bars are set, place the sliced strawberries in a single layer on top of the bars, then return the bars to the fridge to set for an additional 2 hours.

7. Slice into 12 equal-sized bars and serve promptly. (These are best eaten the same day they're prepared, but they can be stored in an airtight container in the fridge for up to 3 days.)

Tip To make these vegan, substitute an equal amount of agar agar for the gelatin.

NUTRITION PER SERVING	233 CALORIES	21.5g TOTAL FAT	7g TOTAL CARBS	5g NET CARBS	5.5g PROTEIN

NUT FREE GLUTEN FREE SUGAR FREE EGG FREE

Coconut Bars

These easy-to-make bars contain only 3 ingredients and can be assembled in less than 5 minutes, but they're dangerously delicious, so be sure you don't eat them all at once!

PREP TIME: **5 MINUTES**   COOK TIME: **NONE**   PASSIVE TIME: **1 HOUR**

MAKES: 6
SERVING SIZE: 1

2 cups (100g/3.5oz) unsweetened desiccated coconut

½ cup (115g/4oz) salted butter, melted

¼ cup (40g/1.2oz) granular erythritol

1. In a large bowl, combine the coconut, butter, and erythritol. Stir well.
2. Line a 8.5 x 5-inch (22 x 13cm) loaf pan with parchment paper. Transfer the mixture to the pan and use a spoon to press it down flat. Transfer to the freezer to set for 1 hour.
3. Cut into 6 equal-sized bars. Store in an airtight container for up to 2 weeks.

Tip I find using a small bread loaf pan works best for these bars. You can use confectioners erythritol if you don't have granular erythritol.

NUTRITION PER SERVING	248 CALORIES	25.5g TOTAL FAT	5.5g TOTAL CARBS	3.3g NET CARBS	1.3g PROTEIN

🍶 **DAIRY FREE** 🌾 **GLUTEN FREE** 🍥 **SUGAR FREE**

"Apple" Pie

There is nothing better than a slice of sweet, flakey apple pie!
Apple, however, isn't keto-friendly, so this recipe utilizes
chayote squash to mimic the texture of apple.

PREP TIME: **20 MINUTES**	COOK TIME: **50 MINUTES**	PASSIVE TIME: **4 HOURS**

MAKES: 12 SERVINGS
SERVING SIZE: 1 SLICE

For the crust

2 cups (7oz/200g) almond flour

¾ cup (2oz/60g) coconut flour

½ tsp xanthan gum

½ tsp baking powder

¼ tsp salt

¼ cup cold water

½ cup (4oz/120g) lard, warmed
   to room temperature

For the filling

4 medium (35oz/1kg) chayote
   squashes, peeled and thinly
   sliced

½ cup (3oz/90g) granular
   erythritol

1 tsp ground cinnamon

zest and juice of 1 lemon

½ tsp guar gum

¼ tsp salt

1 large egg, whisked

1. In a food processor, combine the almond flour, coconut flour, xanthan gum, baking powder, and salt. Pulse until combined, then add the lard in tablespoon-sized chunks and the cold water. Process for 20 seconds or until the ingredients are just combined. Divide the mixture in half and tightly wrap each section in plastic wrap. Transfer to the fridge to chill for a minimum of 2 hours.

2. Preheat the oven to 420°F (220°C). Place the chayote squash slices in a medium pot and cover with water. Bring to a boil over medium heat. Boil for 20 minutes or until the slices become soft but not mushy. Drain the chayote and transfer to a medium bowl. Add the erythritol, cinnamon, lemon zest, lemon juice, guar gum, and salt. Mix well to coat the squash.

3. Place one section of the pie dough between two sheets of parchment paper and roll the dough out into a circle that is 2 inches (5cm) larger than the circumference of a shallow 9-inch (23cm) pie pan. Nest the rolled crust in the pie pan.

4. Place the second half of the dough between two sheets of parchment paper and roll it out into a circle that is large enough to exceed the circumference of the pie pan by 1 inch (2.5cm). Set aside.

5. Spoon the filling into the bottom crust. Carefully place the top crust over the pan, pinch the edges together, and trim away any excess crust. Use a knife to create a small slit in the top of the pie to allow steam to escape. Brush the top of the pie with the whisked egg.

6. Transfer the pie to the oven and bake for 15 minutes, then reduce the temperature to 355°F (180°C) and bake for an additional 30 minutes or until the top turns golden brown. Let the pie cool to room temperature before slicing into 12 equal-sized servings. Store in an airtight container in the fridge for 5 days.

Tip If you can't find chayote squash, you can substitute an equal amount of peeled and sliced jicama.

NUTRITION PER SERVING	//	219 CALORIES	//	20g TOTAL FAT	//	8g TOTAL CARBS	//	5g NET CARBS	//	5g PROTEIN

🌱 **GLUTEN FREE** 🍬 **SUGAR FREE**

Chocolate Coconut Cream Pie

If you're one of those sweet tooths who likes the bitterness of coffee combined with the sweetness of chocolate, this recipe just might become one of your favorites!

PREP TIME: **20 MINUTES** COOK TIME: **10 MINUTES** PASSIVE TIME: **4.5 HOURS**

MAKES: 10 SERVINGS
SERVING SIZE: 1 SLICE

For the crust

1 tsp butter (for greasing)

1 cup (3oz/90g) almond flour

¼ cup (0.8oz/20g) coconut flour

1 tbsp unsweetened cocoa powder

½ tsp salt

1 large egg

2 tbsp coconut oil

¼ tsp stevia extract

For the filling

13.5fl oz (400ml) can chilled coconut cream, clear liquid drained off

⅓ cup (1.8oz/50g) unsweetened baking chocolate

2 tbsp coconut oil

¼ tsp stevia extract

1 tsp vanilla extract

2 tsp instant espresso powder

1 tbsp unsweetened cocoa powder

½ tsp powdered gelatin

1. Preheat the oven to 355°F (180°C), and grease an 8-inch (20cm) pie pan with 1 teaspoon butter

2. Make the crust by combining the almond flour, coconut flour, cocoa powder, and salt in a medium bowl. Mix until a uniform color is achieved. Add the egg, coconut oil, and stevia extract. Mix well to combine.

3. Press the crust mixture into the bottom and sides of the prepared pan, then use a fork to poke holes in the base of the crust. Transfer to the oven and bake for 10 minutes, then remove from the oven and set aside to cool.

4. Combine the coconut cream, baking chocolate, and coconut oil in a medium pan placed over low heat. Heat until the chocolate is just melted, but don't let the ingredients boil. Add the stevia extract, vanilla extract, espresso powder, and cocoa powder. Mix well, then sprinkle the gelatin into the mixture, stir and then remove the pan from the heat.

5. Pour the filling into the pie crust. Let the pie cool for 30 minutes, then cover with plastic wrap and transfer to the fridge to set for a minimum of 4 hours.

6. Cut into 10 equal-sized slices and serve chilled. Store in an airtight container in the fridge for up to 1 week.

Tip To make this vegan, substitute agar agar for the gelatin powder, omit the egg, and add 1 additional tablespoon of coconut oil.

NUTRITION PER SERVING	150 CALORIES	13.5g TOTAL FAT	4.5g TOTAL CARBS	2g NET CARBS	4g PROTEIN

(🐝) **GLUTEN FREE** (🍬) **SUGAR FREE** (🥚) **EGG FREE**

Chocolate Coconut Bounty Bars

As a kid, chocolate bounty bars were one of my absolute favorite sweet treats—the rich, sweet coconut covered with delicious chocolate is incredible! I just had to create a keto-friendly version for all those sweet tooths out there like me.

PREP TIME: **10 MINUTES**   COOK TIME: **NONE**   PASSIVE TIME: **1 HOUR**

MAKES: 6
SERVING SIZE: 1

For the coconut bars

2 cups (3.5oz/100g) unsweetened desiccated coconut

½ cup (4oz/115g) salted butter, melted

¼ cup (1.2oz/40g) granular erythritol

3 tbsp slivered almonds

For the chocolate coating

3oz (90g) unsweetened baking chocolate, chopped

⅛ cup (1oz/30g) salted butter

1. In a large bowl, combine the coconut, melted butter, and erythritol. Stir well to combine.

2. Line a 8.5 x 5-inch (22 x 13cm) loaf pan with parchment paper. Pour the mixture into the pan, and use a spoon to smooth the mixture until flat. Transfer to the freezer to set for a minimum of 1 hour.

3. While the bars are setting, make the chocolate coating by combining the baking chocolate and butter in a heatsafe bowl. Microwave on high until the ingredients are melted, about 2 minutes, then carefully remove the bowl from the microwave and stir until the ingredients are combined.

4. Cut the base into 6 equal-sized bars. Dip the bars in the chocolate, ensuring the chocolate covers the bars completely, then transfer to a cooling rack. Top each bar with equal amounts of the slivered almonds. Store in an airtight container in the freezer for up to 2 weeks.

Tip If you prefer a softer bar, store in the fridge instead of the freezer. (These will keep in the fridge for up to 5 days.)

NUTRITION PER SERVING	383 CALORIES	38.5g TOTAL FAT	10g TOTAL CARBS	6g NET CARBS	3.5g PROTEIN

GLUTEN FREE **SUGAR FREE**

Iced Cinnamon Rolls

These sweet and gooey rolls are made from a unique dough
that combines mozzarella, cream cheese, and almond flour.
It's this unique twist that gives them their fantastic flavor!

PREP TIME: **15 MINUTES**	COOK TIME: **10 MINUTES**	PASSIVE TIME: **25 MINUTES**

MAKES: 12
SERVING SIZE: 3

For the rolls

1½ cups (6oz/170g) preshredded
mozzarella cheese

2 tbsp full-fat cream cheese

1 large egg

¾ cups (70g/2.2oz) almond flour

2 tbsp granular erythritol, divided

1 tsp ground cinnamon

1 tbsp warm water

For the icing

1 tbsp full-fat cream cheese

1 tbsp heavy cream

1 tbsp confectioners erythritol

1. Preheat the oven to 355°F (180°C).

2. Combine the mozzarella and cream cheese in a microwave-safe bowl.
   Heat on high in 30 second increments until the mixture is completely melted,
   about 90 seconds.

3. Add the egg, almond flour, and 1 tablespoon of the erythritol. Mix until the
   ingredients are a uniform color and the texture becomes slightly sticky. Place
   the dough between two sheets of parchment paper and roll it into the shape
   of a rectangle. Place the flattened dough on a large baking pan, transfer to
   the oven to bake for 5 minutes, then set aside to cool for 10 minutes.

4. In a small bowl, combine the remaining erythritol, cinnamon, and water.
   Stir until well combined, then spread the mixture over one side of the
   dough sheet.

5. Starting from one long edge, roll the dough up into a large roll, then cut the
   dough into smaller rolls that are each about the width of 2 fingers. Place the
   rolls on a large baking sheet, rolled sides up, and transfer to the oven to bake
   for an additional 7 minutes.

6. While the rolls are baking, make the icing by combining the cream cheese,
   heavy cream, and erythritol in a small bowl. Mix well, then transfer the
   mixture to a piping bag.

7. Remove the rolls from the oven and let them cool for 15 minutes before
   piping the icing over the top. Store in an airtight container in the fridge for
   up to 5 days.

Tip These rolls are quite small, but they're made mostly of dense cheese, so they will
definitely curb your hunger and satisfy your sweet tooth!

NUTRITION PER SERVING	325 CALORIES	27.5g TOTAL FAT	6g TOTAL CARBS	3.5g NET CARBS	16g PROTEIN

GLUTEN FREE SUGAR FREE EGG FREE

Coffee Cheesecake Bars

These bars combine rich coffee flavor with a creamy
cheesecake texture and my favorite chocolate ganache.

PREP TIME: **15 MINUTES**	COOK TIME: **15 MINUTES**	PASSIVE TIME: **6 HRS 30 MINS**

MAKES: 16
SERVING SIZE: 1

For the base

1 cup (3.5oz/100g) almond flour

⅓ cup (1oz/30g) coconut flour

¼ tsp xanthan gum

2 tbsp granular erythritol

½ tsp baking powder

½ tsp salt

⅓ cup (3oz/90g) cold unsalted
butter

For the filling

2 cups (17.5oz/500g) full-fat cream
cheese

½ cup (4oz/115g) full-fat
sour cream

1 cup (5.5oz/160g) confectioners
erythritol

1 tsp vanilla extract

1 tsp instant espresso powder

2 tsp powdered gelatin

2 tbsp hot water

For the ganache

½ cup (4fl oz/120ml) heavy
whipping cream

1.75oz (50g) unsweetened baking
chocolate, chopped

1. Make the base by combining the almond flour, coconut flour, xanthan gum, erythritol, baking powder, and salt in a food processor. Pulse until well combined, then add the cold butter in tablespoon chunks and process for 20 seconds or until the ingredients are just combined. Tightly wrap the mixture in plastic wrap and transfer to the fridge to chill for a minimum of 2 hours.

2. After 2 hours have elapsed, preheat the oven to 355°F (180°C) and line an 8 x 8-inch (20 x 20cm) baking pan with parchment paper. Remove the base from the fridge, place it between two sheets of parchment paper, and roll it flat enough to fill the bottom of the prepared pan. Place the base in the prepared pan and use a fork to poke holes in the base. Transfer to the oven and bake for 15 minutes, then set aside to cool for 20 minutes.

3. While the base is cooling, make the filling by combining the cream cheese, sour cream, erythritol, and vanilla extract in a large bowl. Use a hand mixer to mix until well combined. Add the espresso and mix until combined.

4. In a small bowl, combine the gelatin and hot water. Stir until the gelatin is completely dissolved, then slowly add the warm gelatin mixture to the cream cheese mixture, while continuously stirring, until the ingredients are combined. Pour the filling over the top of the cooled base. Transfer to the fridge to set for 30 minutes.

5. Make the ganache by adding the whipping cream to a small saucepan placed over medium heat. Heat the cream, stirring continuously until it begins to bubble, then remove the pan from the heat. Place the baking chocolate in a small bowl and pour the hot cream over top of the chocolate. Let it sit for 3 minutes, then stir until a smooth consistency is achieved and no lumps remain.

6. Drizzle the warm ganache over the cooled cheesecake at a diagonal angle, using a back and forth motion. Cover and transfer to the fridge to set for a minimum of 4 hours.

7. Slice into 16 equal-sized bars. Store in an airtight container in the fridge for up to 4 days, or freeze for up to 2 weeks.

NUTRITION PER SERVING	270 CALORIES	26g TOTAL FAT	6g TOTAL CARBS	4g NET CARBS	5g PROTEIN

🌿 GLUTEN FREE 🚫 SUGAR FREE

Pumpkin Pie

This recipe nestles sweet pumpkin in my favorite pie pastry
and features a wonderful combination of spices that
help enhance the flavor of the pumpkin.

PREP TIME: **20 MINUTES**	COOK TIME: **50 MINUTES**	PASSIVE TIME: **4 HOURS**

MAKES: 12 SERVINGS
SERVING SIZE: 1 SLICE

1 Perfect Keto Pie Crust
(see p. 110)

2 cups (17oz/480g) pumpkin purée

2 large eggs

1½ cups (11.5fl oz/345ml) heavy
whipping cream

⅔ cup (3.5oz/100g) granular
erythritol

½ tsp ground cinnamon

1 tsp ground ginger

¼ tsp ground nutmeg

½ tsp salt

1. Preheat the oven to 390°F (200°C).
2. Place the pie dough between two sheets of parchment paper and roll it flat enough to extend at least 2 inches (5cm) beyond the edges of a 10-inch (26cm) pie pan. Nest the dough in the pie pan, crimp the edges, and trim away any excess crust.
3. Cover the edges of the pie crust with foil, and use a fork to poke holes in the base of the crust. Transfer to the oven and bake for 20 minutes.
4. While the crust is baking, make the filling by combining the pumpkin purée, eggs, whipping cream, erythritol, cinnamon, ginger, nutmeg, and salt in a large bowl. Blend with a hand mixer on medium until the ingredients are well combined.
5. Remove the pie crust from the oven and reduce the oven temperature to 355°F (180°C). Spoon the filling into the baked crust. Place the pie in the oven to bake for 40 minutes.
6. Let the baked pie cool completely, cover with plastic wrap, and transfer to the fridge to set for a minimum of 2 hours before slicing into 12 equal-sized servings. Store in an airtight container in the fridge for up to 1 week.

Tip If you're missing a spice, you can substitute 2 teaspoons of a pumpkin spice blend for the cinnamon, ginger, and nutmeg.

NUTRITION PER SERVING	365 CALORIES	33g TOTAL FAT	11g TOTAL CARBS	6g NET CARBS	6.5g PROTEIN

(🌾) **GLUTEN FREE** (🍬) **SUGAR FREE**

Lemon Curd Tart

This delicate, lemony tart features a creamy filling nestled
in a flaky crust. And because it's sugar-free, you'll be reaping
the full benefit of the vitamin C in the lemons.

PREP TIME: **20 MINUTES**	COOK TIME: **25 MINUTES**	PASSIVE TIME: **2 HOURS**

MAKES: 12 SERVINGS
SERVING SIZE: 1 SLICE

For the crust

1 cup (3oz/90g) almond flour

½ cup (1.2oz/40g) coconut flour

¼ tsp xanthan gum

½ tsp baking powder

2 tbsp granular erythritol

¼ tsp salt

⅓ cup (3oz/90g) cold unsalted
   butter, cubed

1 tsp butter (for greasing)

For the curd

3 large eggs

1 large egg yolk

4 lemons, juiced and zested

½ cup (2.4oz/80g) granular
   erythritol

½ cup (4oz/115g) butter

1. Make the crust by combining the almond flour, coconut flour, xanthan gum, baking powder, erythritol, and salt in a food processor. Pulse until combined.

2. Add the cold butter to the food processor in tablespoon-sized chunks. Process for 20 seconds or until the ingredients are just combined, then wrap the mixture tightly in plastic wrap and transfer to the fridge to chill for a minimum of 2 hours.

3. Preheat the oven to 355°F (180°C), and coat the inside of an 8-inch (20cm) tart pan with 1 teaspoon butter.

4. Place the chilled crust between two pieces of parchment paper and roll it flat enough to extend beyond the edges of the tart pan by 2 inches (5cm). Nest the crust in the pan, trim the edges, and use a fork to poke holes in the base of the crust. Transfer to the oven and bake for 15 minutes.

5. While the crust is baking, combine the eggs and egg yolk in a medium bowl. Whisk to combine, then set aside.

6. Place a medium pot of water over low heat, then place a heatproof glass bowl over the top of the pot, making sure the water doesn't touch the bottom of the bowl. Bring the water just to a simmer, then add the lemon juice, lemon zest, erythritol, and butter. Stir continuously until the butter is melted.

7. Once the butter is melted, very slowly add the egg mixture while whisking continuously, making sure the eggs don't overcook and curdle. Continue stirring over low heat just until the mixture coats the back of the spoon, then promptly remove the pan from the heat.

8. Pour the mixture into the baked crust, cover, and transfer to the fridge to set for a minimum of 2 hours. Serve chilled. Cover and store in the fridge for up to 4 days.

Tip For a raspberry tart, substitute 1 cup fresh raspberries for the lemons and lemon zest. For a chocolate tart, substitute 3.5oz (100g) unsweetened baking chocolate for the lemons and lemon zest.

NUTRITION PER SERVING	154 CALORIES	18g TOTAL FAT	3g TOTAL CARBS	2g NET CARBS	3.5g PROTEIN

Ⓓ DAIRY FREE Ⓖ GLUTEN FREE Ⓢ SUGAR FREE Ⓔ EGG FREE

"Apple" Crumble

These single-serving apple crumbles are delicious and easy
to make! Because apple contains too many sugars, this recipe
uses chayote squash, which has a similar texture to apple.

PREP TIME: **10 MINUTES**	COOK TIME: **15 MINUTES**	PASSIVE TIME: **1 HOUR**

MAKES: 2 SERVINGS
SERVING SIZE: 1 (7oz/200g)

2 medium chayote squashes
(approximately 10oz/300g),
peeled and diced

⅓ cup (1.8oz/50g) granular
erythritol

½ tsp ground cinnamon

1 tsp ground ginger

¼ tsp ground nutmeg

6 tbsp finely ground walnuts

2 tbsp sugar-free coconut yogurt

1. Place the chayote in a large pot and cover completely with water. Add the erythritol, cinnamon, ginger, and nutmeg. Bring the ingredients to a boil, then reduce the heat to low and simmer for 5 minutes. Remove the pot from the heat and drain.

2. Divide the chayote between two serving bowls and top each with 3 tablespoons of the ground walnuts and 1 tablespoon of the coconut yogurt.

3. Serve warm, or cover and chill in the fridge for 2 hours prior to serving. Cover with plastic wrap and store in the fridge for up to 4 days.

Tip If you're missing a spice, you can omit the cinnamon, ginger, and nutmeg, and substitute 1¾ teaspoons pumpkin pie spice. If you can't find chayote squash, you can substitute an equal amount of peeled and diced jicama.

NUTRITION PER SERVING	141 CALORIES	11g TOTAL FAT	10g TOTAL CARBS	7g NET CARBS	4g PROTEIN

GLUTEN FREE · SUGAR FREE · EGG FREE

Perfect Keto Pie Crust

This signature keto pie crust is flaky and crispy, and versatile enough to use in a variety of recipes. (This crust is the foundation for many recipes throughout this book.)

PREP TIME: **15 MINUTES**	COOK TIME: **20 MINUTES**	PASSIVE TIME: **2 HOURS**

MAKES: 1 CRUST (445g/15.7oz)
OR 12 SERVINGS

2 cups (7oz/200g) almond flour
¾ cup (2oz/60g) coconut flour
½ tsp xanthan gum
½ tsp baking powder
¼ tsp salt
¾ cup (6oz/180g) unsalted butter, cold

1. In a food processor, combine the almond flour, coconut flour, xanthan gum, baking powder, and salt. Pulse until combined.

2. Add the cold butter in tablespoon-sized chunks. Process for 20 seconds or until the ingredients are just combined. (If you don't have a food processor, you can use two forks to combine the ingredients.)

3. Wrap the mixture tightly in plastic wrap and transfer to the fridge for a minimum of 2 hours, or transfer to the freezer and freeze for up to 2 weeks.

4. When ready to use, roll the thawed dough out flat. Bake for 15 minutes at 355°F (180°C).

Tip To make a crust that does not have to be prebaked, you can substitute 4oz (120g) lard plus ¼ cup water for the butter.

NUTRITION PER SERVING	225 CALORIES	21g TOTAL FAT	6g TOTAL CARBS	3g NET CARBS	4g PROTEIN

⊗ **NUT FREE** ⊛ **GLUTEN FREE** ⊗ **SUGAR FREE**

"Apple" Turnovers

When mixed with erythritol and spices, the chayote squash in this recipe has a similar texture to apple, and it is superior for cooking because it holds its texture when boiled.

| PREP TIME: **20 MINUTES** | COOK TIME: **50 MINUTES** | PASSIVE TIME: **4 HOURS** |

MAKES: 2
SERVING SIZE: ½ TURNOVER

1 medium chayote squash (10oz/300g), peeled and finely diced

½ tsp pumpkin spice blend

¾ cup (4oz/120g) granular erythritol

3 cups (10oz/300g) pre-shredded mozzarella cheese

1 medium egg, warmed to room temperature

10 drops stevia extract

2 tbsp coconut flour

1. In a large pot placed over medium heat, combine the squash and pumpkin spice. Fill the pot with water until the squash is just covered. Bring to a boil, then reduce the heat to low. Simmer for 5 minutes, then remove from the pot from the heat.

2. Drain the squash and transfer to a large bowl. Add the erythritol, stir, and set aside.

3. Preheat the oven to 320°F (160°C). Add the mozzarella to a large, heatsafe bowl and microwave on high for 2 minutes or until melted.

4. Add the egg and stevia extract to the melted mozzarella. Mix thoroughly, then add the coconut flour and continue mixing until a dough forms. (If the dough is too wet to handle, add more coconut flour, in small amounts, and mix until the desired consistency is achieved.)

5. Place the dough between two sheets of parchment paper and roll it out flat enough to form a wide sheet that is approximately .5 inches (1.25cm) thick. (Be careful not to roll the dough too thin; otherwise, it may break when baking.)

6. Divide the dough sheet into two equal-sized sections and place on a large baking sheet. Spoon half the filling into the middle of each dough sheet, fold the edges together, and pinch the edges shut. Use a sharp knife to create a small slit in the top of each turnover to ensure steam can escape.

7. Transfer to the oven and bake for 5 minutes, then use a spatula to flip the turnovers and bake for an additional 5 minutes. Serve warm, or store in an airtight container in the fridge for up to 1 week.

Tip Taste the chayote prior to placing it in the dough to ensure the sweetness is to your liking. If you desire more sweetness, add more erythritol, 1 tablespoon at a time, until the desired sweetness level is reached. If you can't find chayote squash, you can substitute an equal amount of peeled and diced jicama.

| NUTRITION PER SERVING | 295 CALORIES | 20g TOTAL FAT | 7g TOTAL CARBS | 5g NET CARBS | 19g PROTEIN |

① DAIRY FREE ⊛ GLUTEN FREE ⊗ SUGAR FREE

Blueberry Pie

The fresh berries and delicate crust in this homemade classic
will impress any sweet tooth! Lemon zest and cinnamon
help balance the sweetness of the blueberries.

PREP TIME: **15 MINUTES**	COOK TIME: **30 MINUTES**	PASSIVE TIME: **2 HOURS**

MAKES: 12 SERVINGS
SERVING SIZE: 1 SLICE

For the crust

2 cups (7oz/200g) almond flour

½ cup (7oz/60g) coconut flour

½ tsp xanthan gum

½ tsp baking powder

¼ tsp salt

4oz (120g) lard, warmed to room temperature

¼ cup cold water

1 large egg, lightly whisked

For the filling

7oz (200g) fresh blueberries

½ cup (2.4oz/80g) granular erythritol

2 tsp lemon juice

1 tsp lemon zest

½ tsp xanthan gum

¼ tsp ground cinnamon

1. In a food processor, combine the almond flour, coconut flour, xanthan gum, baking powder, and salt. Pulse until combined.

2. Add the lard to the food processor in chunks, then add the cold water. Process for 20 seconds or until the ingredients are just combined. Tightly wrap the mixture in plastic wrap and transfer to the fridge to chill for a minimum 2 hours.

3. Preheat the oven to 320°F (160°C). In a medium bowl, combine the blueberries, erythritol, lemon juice, lemon zest, xanthan gum, and cinnamon. Mix until the contents are just combined and slightly sticky.

4. Divide the chilled pastry dough into 2 evenly-sized pieces. Place one piece of the dough between two sheets of parchment paper and roll it flat enough to extend past the edges of a 9-inch pie pan by 2 inches (5cm). Repeat with the second piece.

5. Remove the top sheet of parchment paper from the first piece of dough. Place the pie tin upside down and on top of the pastry, then simultaneously flip both upright so the pie pastry now sits inside the pie pan.

6. Pour the filling into the pie pan, place the second pastry sheet on top, and pinch the edges of the dough sheets together. (Alternatively, you can create a lattice pattern in the top crust by cross hatching ¾-inch [2cm] strips of the pastry.) Brush the top of the pie with the whisked egg.

7. Transfer to the oven, bake for 15 minutes, then increase the oven temperature to 355°F (180°C) and bake for an additional 15 minutes. Transfer to the fridge to cool for at least 1 hour before serving. Cover with plastic wrap and store in the fridge for up to 5 days.

Tip If you don't have lard, you can substitute 6oz (180g) butter, but the texture will be more more crumbly and the dough will be slightly more difficult to work with.

NUTRITION PER SERVING	217 CALORIES	19g TOTAL FAT	8g TOTAL CARBS	4g NET CARBS	4g PROTEIN

🌾 **GLUTEN FREE** 🍬 **SUGAR FREE** 🥚 **EGG FREE**

Chocolate Hazelnut Pie

This scrumptious chocolate hazelnut pie has a no-bake filling and sets up very nicely in the fridge, and the toasted hazelnuts provide a familiar hazelnut spread flavor.

PREP TIME: **15 MINUTES**	COOK TIME: **15 MINUTES**	PASSIVE TIME: **1 HR 40 MINS**

MAKES: 12 SERVINGS
SERVING SIZE: 1 SLICE

For the crust

2 cups (7oz/200g) almond flour

¾ cup (2oz/60g) coconut flour

½ tsp xanthan gum

½ tsp baking powder

¼ tsp salt

¾ cup (6oz/180g) unsalted butter, cold

For the filling

1 cup (4oz/150g) raw hazelnuts

1 cup (8.8oz/250g) full-fat cream cheese

⅓ cup (3oz/90g) full-fat sour cream

3 tbsp unsweetened cocoa powder

½ tsp salt

1 tsp lemon juice

2 tsp vanilla extract

½ tbsp powdered gelatin

½ cup (2.5oz/70g) granular erythritol

⅓ cup (3fl oz/90ml) hot water

1 cup (8fl oz/240ml) heavy whipping cream

1. Make the crust by combining the almond flour, coconut flour, xanthan gum, baking powder, and salt in a food processor. Pulse until combined, then add the cold butter in tablespoon-sized chunks and process for 20 seconds or until the ingredients are just combined. Tightly wrap the mixture in plastic wrap and transfer to the fridge to chill for a minimum of 1 hour.

2. Preheat the oven to 355°F (180°C). Spread the hazelnuts across a large baking sheet and place in the oven to toast for 10 minutes. Remove from the oven and set aside to cool.

3. Place the chilled crust between two sheets of plastic wrap and roll it flat enough to extend 1 inch (2.5cm) beyond the edges of a 9-inch (23cm) pie pan. Nest the crust inside the pie pan and use a fork to poke holes in the base. Transfer to the oven and bake for 15 minutes.

4. While the crust is baking, remove the skins from the hazelnuts by squeezing them between your thumb and index finger (the skins should slip off quite easily). Transfer the hazelnuts to a food processor and grind until the nuts form a fine paste.

5. Remove the crust from the oven and set aside to cool for 10 minutes. In a large bowl, combine the ground hazelnuts, cream cheese, sour cream, cocoa powder, salt, lemon juice, and vanilla extract. Mix until combined.

6. In a small bowl, combine the gelatin, erythritol, and hot water. Stir until the ingredients are completely dissolved, then add the mixture to the cream cheese mixture. Using a hand mixer, mix until the ingredients are well combined and no lumps remain.

7. In a second bowl, beat the heavy whipping cream just until soft peaks form. Gently fold the whipped cream into the cream cheese mixture.

8. Spoon the filling into the pie crust and transfer to the fridge to set for a minimum of 2 hours. Serve chilled. Cover with plastic wrap and store in the fridge for up to 5 days.

NUTRITION PER SERVING	//	328 CALORIES	//	31g TOTAL FAT	//	8g TOTAL CARBS	//	4.5g NET CARBS	//	7.3g PROTEIN

🌾 **GLUTEN FREE** 🍬 **SUGAR FREE**

Lemon Meringue Pie

If you love the combination of zesty lemon and sweet meringue, this sweet and tart pie will be the perfect dessert.

PREP TIME: **15 MINUTES**   COOK TIME: **20 MINUTES**   PASSIVE TIME: **6 HOURS**

MAKES: 12 SERVINGS
SERVING SIZE: 1 SLICE

1 Perfect Keto Pie Crust
   (see p. 110)

For the filling

1⅓ cups (10.5fl oz/315ml) heavy
   whipping cream

¾ cup granular erythritol

½ cup lemon juice (about
   4 lemons)

1 tbsp freshly grated lemon zest

3 tbsp powdered gelatin

2 tbsp hot water

4 egg yolks

For the meringue

4 egg whites

¼ cup (30g/1oz) powdered
   erythritol

1. Make the filling by combining the whipping cream and erythritol in a medium saucepan placed over medium heat. Stir until the erythritol is completely dissolved, then remove the pan from the heat. Add the lemon juice and lemon zest. Stir.

2. Combine the hot water and gelatin in small bowl and stir until the gelatin dissolves completely, about 3 minutes. Add the gelatin mixture to the warm filling mixture and stir until well combined. Let the mixture cool slightly, about 10 minutes.

3. Add the egg yolks to the mixture, one at a time, while continuously whisking and ensuring the ingredients are well combined before adding each additional egg. Place the pan back over low heat. Cook, stirring continuously, until the mixture thickens, then remove the pan from the heat.

4. Preheat the oven to 320°F (160°C). Place the pie crust between two pieces of parchment paper and roll it flat enough to exceed the edges of a 9-inch (23 cm) pie pan by about 2 inches (5cm). Remove the top sheet of parchment paper and place the pie pan upside down and on top of the pastry. Flip both upright so that the pie pastry is nested inside the pie pan. Use a fork to poke holes in the base of the crust, then transfer to the oven and bake for 20 minutes. Pour the filling into the baked crust. Set aside.

5. Make the meringue by placing the egg whites in a medium bowl. Whip just until stiff peaks form, then add the erythritol and stir to combine. Spoon the meringue over the filling, and use the back of the spoon to spread the meringue evenly across the surface of the filling and then use the back of the spoon to "pull" high peaks from the surface of the meringue.

6. Using a kitchen torch, lightly brown the peaks of the meringue (alternatively, place the pie under the broiler for 5 minutes, or until the peaks just begin to lightly brown).

7. Transfer the pie to the fridge to cool for a minimum of 6 hours. Cut into 12 equal-sized slices, serve chilled. Store in an airtight container in the fridge for up to 5 days.

NUTRITION PER SERVING	225 CALORIES	21g TOTAL FAT	6g TOTAL CARBS	3g NET CARBS	4g PROTEIN

🌾 **GLUTEN FREE** 🚫 **SUGAR FREE**

Key Lime Pie

This light and delectable key lime pie is made without condensed milk, which is traditionally used in key lime pie.

PREP TIME: **15 MINUTES**	COOK TIME: **1 HOUR**	PASSIVE TIME: **2 HOURS**

MAKES: 12 SERVINGS
SERVING SIZE: 1 SLICE

For the crust

2 cups (7oz/200g) almond flour

¾ cup (2oz/60g) coconut flour

½ tsp xanthan gum

½ tsp baking powder

¼ tsp salt

¾ cup (6oz/180g) cold unsalted butter

For the filling

2¼ cups (17fl oz/500ml) heavy cream, divided

2 tbsp (1oz/30g) unsalted butter

½ cup (2.8fl oz/80g) granular erythritol, divided

zest and juice of 4 limes

4 large eggs, warmed to room temperature

1 tsp vanilla extract

1. Make the crust by combining the almond flour, coconut flour, xanthan gum, baking powder, and salt in a food processor. Pulse until combined.

2. Add the butter to the food processor in tablespoon-sized chunks. Process for 20 seconds or until the ingredients are just combined. (If you don't have a food processor, you can use two forks to mash the ingredients together). Tightly wrap the mixture in plastic wrap and transfer to the fridge to chill for a minimum 2 hours.

3. While the crust is cooling, combine 1½ cups of the heavy cream, butter, and ¼ cup of the erythritol in a medium pan placed over medium heat. Stir the mixture continuously until the erythritol is dissolved, then reduce the heat to low and let the mixture simmer for 30 minutes. Remove from the heat and set aside cool.

4. In a large bowl, combine the remaining heavy cream, remaining erythritol, lime zest, lime juice, eggs, and vanilla extract. Slowly add the heated cream and butter mixture, stirring continuously, until the ingredients are well combined.

5. Preheat the oven to 320°F (160°C). Place the chilled pie crust dough between two sheets of parchment paper and roll it flat enough to extend past the edges of a 9.5-inch (24cm) pie pan by about 2 inches (5cm).

6. Remove the top sheet of parchment paper. Place the pie pan upside-down on top of the pastry dough sheet, then flip both right-side-up so the pie pastry is nested inside the pie pan. Use a fork to poke holes in the base of the crust. Transfer to the oven and bake for 20 minutes.

7. Pour the filling into the baked crust. Place the pie back in the oven to bake for an additional 40 minutes or until the center of the pie is firm.

8. Transfer the pie to the refrigerator to cool for a minimum of 1 hour prior to slicing into 12 equal-sized servings. Cover with plastic wrap and store in the fridge for up to 4 days.

Tip For a crust that does not need to be prebaked, substitute 4oz (120g) lard and ¼ cup water for the butter.

NUTRITION PER SERVING	350 CALORIES	33g TOTAL FAT	8g TOTAL CARBS	4.5g NET CARBS	7.2g PROTEIN

CHAPTER 6

Confections and Fat Bombs

Feeling the urge for something a little more rich and decadent? These sweet confections and super-satisfying fat bombs will curb your craving, no matter when it hits!

GLUTEN FREE ⊛ SUGAR FREE ⊘ EGG FREE

Peanut Butter Cups

These easy-to-make, sweet and salty treats combine peanut butter and chocolate to create a confection that mimics the sugary, store-bought versions! You'll find yourself making these little gems much more often than you think.

PREP TIME: **20 MINUTES**   COOK TIME: **NONE**   PASSIVE TIME: **1 HOUR**

MAKES: 9
SERVING SIZE: 1

4oz (120g) unsweetened dark chocolate

½ cup (3.5oz/100g) salted butter

4 tbsp all-natural, sugar-free peanut butter

1. Combine the chocolate and butter in a heatsafe bowl and microwave on high until the ingredients are melted, about 2 minutes. Carefully remove the bowl from the microwave and stir until the ingredients are combined and no lumps remain.

2. Insert 9 cupcake liners into a large cupcake tray. Pour half the warm mixture into the cupcake molds and transfer the cups to the freezer to set for 30 minutes.

3. Remove the cups from the freezer and place equal-sized dollops of the peanut butter on top of each base layer, making sure the peanut butter doesn't touch the sides of the molds.

4. Pour the remaining warm chocolate over top of the peanut butter (reheat the chocolate in the microwave if it's too difficult to pour). Place the cups back in the freezer to set for an additional 30 minutes before serving. Store in an airtight container in the freezer for up to 1 month.

Tip To make almond butter cups, substitute an equal amount of all-natural, sugar-free almond butter for the peanut butter.

NUTRITION PER SERVING	283 CALORIES	30g TOTAL FAT	8.5g TOTAL CARBS	5.5g NET CARBS	5g PROTEIN

ⓧ **NUT FREE** ⓖ **GLUTEN FREE** ⓢ **SUGAR FREE** ⓔ **EGG FREE**

Peppermint Patties

Peppermint patties were made popular back in the 1940s.
This keto version contains plenty of healthy fats, and the taste
closely mimics the original version of the famous dark
chocolate-covered peppermint confection.

PREP TIME: **20 MINUTES**	COOK TIME: **90 SECONDS**	PASSIVE TIME: **1 HR 30 MINS**

MAKES: 9
SERVING SIZE: 1

4 tbsp coconut oil

¼ tsp peppermint extract

1 tbsp confectioners erythritol

½ cup (3.5oz/100g) unsalted butter

4oz (120g) unsweetened dark
   chocolate

1. Insert 12 baking liners into a large cupcake tray.

2. In a small bowl, combine the coconut oil, peppermint extract, and erythritol. Stir to combine, then spoon even amounts of the mixture into six of the cupcake molds.

3. Combine the butter and chocolate in a heatsafe glass bowl. Microwave on high until the ingredients are melted, about 90 seconds, then remove from the microwave and stir until the ingredients are combined and no lumps remain.

4. Let the chocolate mixture cool slightly, then transfer half the mixture to the remaining six cupcake molds. Place the tray in the freezer until the ingredients are just set, about 15 minutes.

5. Once set, remove the peppermint sections from the cupcake molds and place them on the top of the chocolate molds. Fill the molds with the remaining chocolate mixture.

6. Transfer the patties in the freezer to set for a minimum of 1 hour. Store in an airtight container in the fridge for up to 1 week, or freeze for up to 2 weeks.

Tip For some other unique flavors, try substituting equal amounts of strawberry, almond, or banana extracts for the peppermint extract.

NUTRITION PER SERVING	300 CALORIES	33g TOTAL FAT	6g TOTAL CARBS	3.5g NET CARBS	2.5g PROTEIN

GLUTEN FREE **SUGAR FREE** **EGG FREE**

Peanut Butter and Jelly Fat Bombs

Peanut butter and jelly (or what we call *jam* in Australia)
paired with chocolate is a devine flavor combination—
think creamy, salty, sweet goodness in a bite-sized
serving to create the perfect on-the-go treat!

PREP TIME: **15 MINUTES**   COOK TIME: **15 MINUTES**   PASSIVE TIME: **1 HOUR**

MAKES: 9
SERVING SIZE: 1

For the base layer

½ cup (2.5oz/100g) unsalted butter

3 tbsp unsweetened cocoa
   powder

2 tsp granular erythritol

Pinch of salt

For the top layer

1 cup (2.5oz/100g) raspberries
   (fresh or frozen)

1 tbsp granular erythritol

½ tsp powdered gelatin

4 tbsp water

Pinch of salt

⅓ cup (2.5oz/100g) no-sugar-
   added, all-natural peanut
   butter

1. In a medium pan placed over medium heat, combine the butter, cocoa powder, erythritol, and salt. Stir until the erythritol is dissolved and the ingredients are well combined, then divide the mixture between 9 sections of a silicone mini-cupcake tray. Transfer to the freezer to set for 20 minutes.

2. While the base layers are setting, combine the raspberries, erythritol, gelatin, water, and salt in a medium pan placed over medium heat. Heat until the mixture thickens, then transfer to a fine mesh sieve placed over a glass bowl. Strain, discard the solids, then set aside to cool for 15 minutes.

3. Spoon the peanut butter over the hardened chocolate layers, using the back of the spoon to smooth the peanut butter until it's level. Place the tray back in the freezer for an additional 20 minutes.

4. Pour the jelly mixture over the set base layers. Transfer to the fridge to set for 20 minutes, then remove the bombs from the molds and transfer to an airtight container. Store in the fridge for up to 1 week, or freeze for up to 2 weeks.

Tip Allow frozen fat bombs to thaw at room temperature for 15 minutes before consuming.

NUTRITION PER SERVING // 257 CALORIES // 25g TOTAL FAT // 9g TOTAL CARBS // 5g NET CARBS // 4g PROTEIN

🌾 **GLUTEN FREE** 🍬 **SUGAR FREE** ⊘ **EGG FREE**

Mixed Berry Cream Cheese Fat Bombs

Fat bombs are perfect as a dessert or a super-filling snack,
and these fruity cream cheese bombs are an absolute delight.
Because berries contain more water and fiber than most
other fruits, they're still acceptable for keto sweets.

| PREP TIME: **10 MINUTES** | COOK TIME: **NONE** | PASSIVE TIME: **4 HRS 30 MINS** |

MAKES: 12
SERVING SIZE: 1

For the base layer
⅔ cup (4oz/150g) full-fat cream cheese

½ stick (1.8oz/50g) unsalted butter, melted

1 tbsp granular erythritol

1 tsp vanilla extract

¼ cup (1.8oz/50g) refined coconut oil

7 fresh strawberries

For the top layer
½ cup (3.2oz/100g) refined coconut oil

⅓ cup (1.2oz/50g) fresh blueberries

2 tsp granular erythritol

1. Make the base layer by combining the cream cheese, butter, erythritol, vanilla extract, and coconut oil in a medium bowl. Use a hand mixer to blend until the ingredients are well combined.

2. Add the strawberries to a blender and blend on high until a smooth consistency is achieved and no lumps remain. Add the strawberries to the cream cheese mixture and stir until the ingredients are well combined.

3. Evenly divide the base layer into 12 sections of a silicone mini-cupcake tray, filling each section approximately three quarters full. Use a teaspoon to smooth the tops, then transfer to the freezer to set for 20 minutes or until the mixture becomes firm.

4. While the base layer is cooling, make the top layer by combining the coconut oil, blueberries, and erythritol in a blender. Blend until a smooth consistency is achieved and no lumps remain.

5. Pour the top layer mixture over the set base layers. Return the bombs to the freezer to set for a minimum of 4 hours. Store in an airtight container in the freezer for up to 2 weeks.

Tip If you don't have refined coconut oil, you can substitute regular coconut oil, but the coconut taste will be more pronounced.

| NUTRITION PER SERVING | 202 CALORIES | 21g TOTAL FAT | 2.1g TOTAL CARBS | 1.8g NET CARBS | 1g PROTEIN |

⊗ **NUT FREE** ⊛ **GLUTEN FREE** ⊛ **SUGAR FREE**

Chocolate-covered Cheesecake Fat Bombs

These distinctive fat bombs have a soft and creamy cheesecake base and a crisp chocolate top layer that will have you immediately wanting more! This is one of the most popular recipes on my FatForWeightLoss blog.

PREP TIME: **10 MINUTES**	COOK TIME: **NONE**	PASSIVE TIME: **4 HRS 30 MINS**

MAKES: 12
SERVING SIZE: 1

For the base layer

⅔ cup (4oz/150g) full-fat cream cheese

½ stick (1.8oz/50g) butter, melted

1 tbsp confectioners erythritol

1 tsp vanilla extract

¼ cup (1.8oz/50g) refined coconut oil, melted

For the top layer

½ cup (3.2oz/100g) refined coconut oil, melted

1 tsp unsweetened cocoa powder

2 tsp confectioners erythritol

1. Make the base layer by combining the cream cheese, butter, erythritol, vanilla extract, and coconut oil in a medium bowl. Use a hand mixer to mix until the ingredients are well combined.

2. Evenly divide the base layer into 12 sections of a silicone mini-cupcake tray. Use a spoon to smooth the tops, then place the tray in the freezer for 20 minutes or until the mixture is mostly firm.

3. While the base layer is setting, make the chocolate top layer by combining the coconut oil, cocoa powder, and erythritol in a medium bowl. Mix until the ingredients are well combined.

4. Pour the chocolate mixture over the partially set base layers and return the fat bombs to the freezer to set for a minimum of 4 hours. Store in an airtight container in the freezer for up to 2 weeks.

Tip If you don't have refined coconut oil, you can substitute regular coconut oil, but the coconut flavor will be more pronounced.

NUTRITION PER SERVING	196 CALORIES	21g TOTAL FAT	2g TOTAL CARBS	1g NET CARBS	1g PROTEIN

DAIRY FREE ⊘ NUT FREE ⊘ GLUTEN FREE ⊘ SUGAR FREE ⊘ EGG FREE

Dark Chocolate

Most store-bought dark chocolate contains sugar or doesn't
have enough fat content to be truly appropriate for a
ketogenic diet. This recipe is keto-friendly and is great
as a sweet treat or for use as a base for other recipes.

PREP TIME: **15 MINUTES**	COOK TIME: **1 MINUTE**	PASSIVE TIME: **1 HOUR**

MAKES: 12 SERVINGS
SERVING SIZE: 1 PIECE

½ cup (4fl oz/115ml) coconut oil

4oz (120g) cocoa butter, grated

½ tsp vanilla bean paste (or 1 tsp
   vanilla extract)

¼ tsp salt

20 drops stevia extract

½ cup (2oz/60g) unsweetened
   cocoa powder

¼ cup (1oz/30g) unsweetened
   cacao nibs

¼ tsp salt flakes (optional)

1. Place the coconut oil in a heatsafe bowl. Microwave on high for 1 minute, then add the grated cocoa butter. Stir until the cocoa butter is completely melted into the coconut oil.

2. Add the vanilla bean paste, salt, and stevia extract. Stir until well combined.

3. Add the cocoa powder and cacao nibs. Stir until the ingredients are well combined.

4. Line a large cupcake tray with 12 small cupcake liners. Fill each cup with equal amounts of the mixture. Sprinkle the salt flakes over top, if using.

5. Transfer to the fridge to set for 1 hour and then remove the pieces from the molds. Store in an airtight container in the fridge for up to 2 weeks.

Tip For different flavor combinations, try adding a small pinch of chili powder or add ⅛ teaspoon of peppermint, coconut, or espresso extracts.

NUTRITION PER SERVING	195 CALORIES	21g TOTAL FAT	3g TOTAL CARBS	1g NET CARBS	1.5g PROTEIN

GLUTEN FREE ⊗ SUGAR FREE ⊘ EGG FREE

Chocolate Espresso Truffles

There are so many different types of truffle chocolates, but nearly all of them are unsuitable for a keto diet because of the high sugar content. These decadent truffles, however, are divine, and they also happen to be keto friendly!

PREP TIME: **10 MINUTES**   COOK TIME: **NONE**   PASSIVE TIME: **2 HOURS**

MAKES: 9
SERVING SIZE: 1

¼ cup (1oz/30g) unsweetened cocoa powder

¼ cup (2fl oz/60ml) coconut oil

¼ cup (1oz/30g) almond flour

2 tbsp coconut flour

2 tbsp heavy whipping cream

2 tsp granular erythritol

1 tsp instant espresso powder

1 tbsp hot water

2 tbsp unsweetened cocoa powder (for dusting)

1. In a medium bowl, combine the cocoa powder, coconut oil, almond flour, coconut flour, whipping cream, and erythritol. Stir until the ingredients are well combined.

2. Combine the espresso powder and hot water in a small bowl. Stir until the expresso powder dissolves completely, then add to the almond flour mixture. Stir to combine.

3. Spoon the mixture out into 9 equal-sized portions, then roll the portions into equal-sized balls. Place the cocoa powder on a small plate and roll the balls in the cocoa powder.

4. Place the truffles in mini-cupcake liners and transfer to the fridge to set for a minimum of 2 hours. Store in an airtight container in the fridge for up to 5 days.

Tip If the mixture is too soft to roll into balls, place it in the fridge for 5–10 minutes to allow the coconut oil to harden slightly.

NUTRITION PER SERVING	95 CALORIES	9.3g TOTAL FAT	3g TOTAL CARBS	1.2g NET CARBS	1.4g PROTEIN

DAIRY FREE ⓘ GLUTEN FREE ⓘ SUGAR FREE ⓘ EGG FREE

Chocolate Fudge

Traditional fudge is made with condensed milk, but this easy-
to-make fudge uses peanut butter and coconut oil to help
make it healthier and also help enhance the fudgy flavor.

PREP TIME: **5 MINUTES**	COOK TIME: **NONE**	PASSIVE TIME: **30 MINUTES**

MAKES: 8 SERVINGS
SERVING SIZE: 1 PIECE

½ cup (4oz/120g) all-natural, sugar-free peanut butter

¼ cup (1.2oz/40g) coconut oil

3 tbsp unsweetened cocoa powder

¼ tsp vanilla extract

20 drops stevia extract

Pinch of sea salt

1. In a large mixing bowl, combine the peanut butter, coconut oil, vanilla extract, and cocoa powder. Stir until well combined.

2. Add the stevia, 5 drops at a time, stirring the mixture each time, until the stevia is fully integrated into the mixture.

3. Add the sea salt, stir, then transfer the mixture to 8 ice cube tray cups. Transfer to the freezer to set for 1 hour. Store in an airtight container in the freezer for up to 1 week.

Tip If desired, an equal amount of almond butter can be substituted for the peanut butter. For a different flavor, eliminate the vanilla extract and stevia extract and add ¼ teaspoon hazelnut-flavored stevia extract.

NUTRITION PER SERVING	//	140 CALORIES	//	13g TOTAL FAT	//	4.5g TOTAL CARBS	//	3g NET CARBS	//	4g PROTEIN

Ⓓ **DAIRY FREE** Ⓝ **NUT FREE** Ⓖ **GLUTEN FREE** Ⓢ **SUGAR FREE** Ⓔ **EGG FREE**

Gummy Candies

These soft, chewy confections are tasty and contain a wealth of health-promoting properties. Gelatin helps keep joints healthy and also can help improve gut health.

PREP TIME: **15 MINUTES**	COOK TIME: **NONE**	PASSIVE TIME: **3 HOURS**

MAKES: 12
SERVING SIZE: 3

1 tea bag berry-flavored herbal tea

½ cup (4 fl oz/115ml) hot water

2 tbsp powdered gelatin

2 tbsp granular erythritol

1. Place the tea bag in the hot water and steep for 2–3 minutes.

2. Remove the tea bag and add the gelatin and erythritol. Stir continuously until the ingredients are completely dissolved.

3. Divide the mixture between 12 equal-sized candy molds, then transfer to the fridge to set for a minimum of 3 hours. Store in an airtight container in the fridge for up to 1 week.

Tip Any fruit-flavored herbal tea, such as mixed berry, black cherry, or strawberry, will work, but you also can experiment with flavors like peppermint or spearmint, or you can use a green tea. (For a keto-friendly jelly, just add 1 additional cup of hot water and refrigerate until set.)

NUTRITION PER SERVING	12 CALORIES	0g TOTAL FAT	0g TOTAL CARBS	0g NET CARBS	3g PROTEIN

⊗ **NUT FREE** ⊛ **GLUTEN FREE** ⊛ **SUGAR FREE** ⊘ **EGG FREE**

Caramel Sauce

A good caramel sauce is creamy, sweet, and punchy, and is the perfect accompaniment to cold desserts and cakes. This easy recipe is delicious served warm over vanilla ice cream!

PREP TIME: **5 MINUTES**   COOK TIME: **15 MINUTES**   PASSIVE TIME: **30 MINUTES**

MAKES: 20 SERVINGS
SERVING SIZE:
1 TABLESPOON

¾ cup (6.8oz/200g) unsalted butter

1 cup (8.5fl oz/250ml) heavy whipping cream

½ cup (3oz/90g) granular erythritol

1 tsp vanilla extract

¼ tsp salt

¼ tsp citric acid powder

1. Add the butter to a medium saucepan placed over medium heat. Heat until the butter just begins to brown.
2. Add the heavy cream and erythritol. Continue stirring until the mixture begins to boil, then add the vanilla extract, salt, and citric acid powder. Stir and remove the pan from the heat to allow the mixture to cool to room temperature, about 30 minutes.
3. Using an immersion blender, blend until a smooth texture is achieved. Store in an airtight container in the fridge for up to 1 week.

Tip The citric acid accentuates the sweetness of the caramel and balances the salt. If you don't have citric acid powder, you can substitute 1 teaspoon lemon juice.

NUTRITION PER SERVING	109 CALORIES	12.5g TOTAL FAT	0.5g TOTAL CARBS	0.5g NET CARBS	0.5g PROTEIN

GLUTEN FREE **SUGAR FREE** **EGG FREE**

Sweet Almond Fat Bombs

These sweet and nutty treats are my take on marzipan—
an aromatic almond paste used in fruitcakes and wedding
cakes. These fat bombs are not high in sugar like traditional
marzipan, but they taste every bit as good!

PREP TIME: **15 MINUTES**	COOK TIME: **NONE**	PASSIVE TIME: **2 HOURS**

MAKES: 9
SERVING SIZE: 1

1 cup (2.6oz/75g) blanched almonds

¼ cup (1oz/30g) confectioners erythritol

1 tbsp coconut oil

¼ tsp almond extract

½ tsp rose water (optional)

4 tbsp unsweetened desiccated coconut, divided

2 tbsp salted butter, cold

1. Add the almonds to a food processor and process until finely ground.

2. Add the erythritol, coconut oil, almond extract, rose water (if using), 2 tablespoons of the desiccated coconut, and butter to the food processor. Process until a thick, uniform paste is formed.

3. Divide the mixture into 9 equal-sized pieces and then roll the pieces into balls. Place the remaining coconut on a plate and roll the balls in the coconut until completely coated. Transfer to an airtight container and store in the fridge for up to 1 week.

Tip An equal amount of rum can be substituted for the rose water. If you don't have blanched almonds, soak whole, unsalted almonds in hot water for 5 minutes, then pinch to remove the skins.

NUTRITION PER SERVING	109 CALORIES	10g TOTAL FAT	2.5g TOTAL CARBS	1g NET CARBS	2g PROTEIN

GLUTEN FREE SUGAR FREE EGG FREE

Rum Balls

These festive, truffle-like treats pack a flavorful punch
because they aren't baked, so the alcohol is retained.
While traditional rum balls contain rum, this recipe also can
be made with an alcohol-free rum extract.

PREP TIME: **15 MINUTES**	COOK TIME: **NONE**	PASSIVE TIME: **2 HOURS**

MAKES: 9
SERVING SIZE: 1

¼ cup (1oz/30g) cocoa powder

¼ cup (2fl oz/60ml) coconut oil

¼ cup (1oz/30g) almond flour

2 tbsp coconut flour

2 tbsp heavy whipping cream

2 tsp granular erythritol

2 tbsp (1fl oz/30ml) dark rum

¾ cup (2.8oz/75g) desiccated
   coconut, divided

1. In a large bowl, combine the cocoa powder, coconut oil, almond flour, coconut flour, whipping cream, erythritol, rum, and ½ cup of the desiccated coconut. Mix until the ingredients are well combined and form a sticky texture.

2. Divide the mixture into 9 equal-sized portions. Roll the portions into balls.

3. Place the remaining desiccated coconut on a small plate. Roll each ball in the mixture until completely coated in the coconut.

4. Transfer the rum balls to an airtight container and place in the fridge to set for a minimum of 2 hours. Store in the fridge for up to 1 week.

Tip To make an alcohol-free version, substitute 1 teaspoon alcohol-free rum extract for the rum.

NUTRITION PER SERVING	146 CALORIES	13.5g TOTAL FAT	4g TOTAL CARBS	1.5g NET CARBS	2g PROTEIN

CHAPTER 7

Frozen Desserts

No keto sweet tooth would ever be satisfied without some frozen treats on the menu! Get ready for ice creams, shakes, smoothies, sorbet, and much more.

🌾 **GLUTEN FREE** 🍬 **SUGAR FREE**

Mint Chocolate Shake

If you're a fan of mint and chocolate, you're going to love this shake! Creamy ice cream is combined with decadent, rich cocoa and bright mint. It's the perfect cool treat for a summer day, and you'll never believe it's sugar free!

PREP TIME: **5 MINUTES**   COOK TIME: **NONE**   PASSIVE TIME: **NONE**

MAKES: 1 SERVING
SERVING SIZE: 8FL OZ (240ml)

1 cup (6oz/170g) Vanilla Ice Cream (see p. 148)

⅓ cup (2.7fl oz/80ml) unsweetened almond milk

2 tsp unsweetened cocoa powder

¼ tsp peppermint extract

¼ tsp dried mint leaves

1. Combine the ingredients in a large blender.
2. Blend on high for 1 minute or until the mixture is smooth and creamy. Serve promptly.

Tip For an extra-rich treat, top with ½ cup whipped cream and dust with a little extra cocoa powder. (Nutrition with whipped cream: 595 calories, 60g total fat, 8g total carbs, 6g net carbs, and 9g protein.)

NUTRITION PER SERVING	390 CALORIES	38g TOTAL FAT	7g TOTAL CARBS	5g NET CARBS	7g PROTEIN

DAIRY FREE · GLUTEN FREE · SUGAR FREE · EGG FREE

Strawberry Avocado Smoothie

With so many decadent sweets, sometimes a simple, clean
smoothie might be just what you're looking for. This recipe
has a smooth, creamy texture with a slight ginger kick that
will help get your morning off to a healthy start.

PREP TIME: **5 MINUTES** COOK TIME: **NONE** PASSIVE TIME: **NONE**

MAKES: 2 SERVINGS
SERVING SIZE: 11FL OZ
(320ml)

½ large avocado, sliced

½ cup (75g/2.3oz) fresh
strawberries, sliced

¼ cup (5g/0.15oz) fresh mint,
roughly chopped

1 thumb-sized piece of fresh
ginger, thinly sliced

½ tsp ground cinnamon

¼ tsp ground cardamom

Juice of ½ lime

2 cups (15.5fl oz/460ml)
unsweetened almond milk

1. Combine the ingredients in a large blender.
2. Blend on high for 1 minute or until the mixture is smooth and creamy.
   Serve promptly.

Tip Garnish the top of the glass with a few whole strawberries or wet the inside of
the glass and place a few thinly sliced strawberries on the sides of the glass prior
to pouring the smoothie into the glass.

NUTRITION PER SERVING	112 CALORIES	8g TOTAL FAT	8.5g TOTAL CARBS	5.5g NET CARBS	2.5g PROTEIN

⊕ **GLUTEN FREE** ⊛ **SUGAR FREE**

Vanilla Cinnamon Shake

This rich and creamy shake is the perfect thickness and features a yummy blend of creamy ice cream and warm cinnamon. And with healthy fats and no sugar, it's keto friendly and will make your tummy happy!

PREP TIME: **5 MINUTES**	COOK TIME: **NONE**	PASSIVE TIME: **NONE**

MAKES: 1 SERVING
SERVING SIZE: 8FL OZ (240ml)

1 cup (6oz/170g) Vanilla Ice Cream (see p. 148)

⅓ cup (2.7fl oz/80ml) unsweetened almond milk

1 tsp vanilla extract

¼ tsp ground cinnamon

¼ tsp ground nutmeg

Small pinch of salt

1. Combine the ingredients in a large cup or blender.
2. Using a high-speed blender or stick blender, blend on high for 1 minute or until the mixture becomes smooth and creamy. Serve promptly.

Tip For an extra rich treat, top with ½ cup whipped cream. (Nutrition with whipped cream: 600 calories, 60g total fat, 7g total carbs, 6g net carbs, and 8g protein.)

NUTRITION PER SERVING	400 CALORIES	38g TOTAL FAT	6g TOTAL CARBS	5g NET CARBS	7g PROTEIN

DAIRY FREE **NUT FREE** **GLUTEN FREE** **SUGAR FREE** **EGG FREE**

Blueberry Smoothie

Smoothies typically are made from an abundance of summer
fruits and berries, which also tend to pack in a lot of hidden
sugar. This keto smoothie limits the sugar and will help
you stay under your carb limit for the day.

PREP TIME: **5 MINUTES**	COOK TIME: **NONE**	PASSIVE TIME: **NONE**

MAKES: 1 SERVING
SERVING SIZE: 13.5FL OZ
(400ml)

¾ cup (6.7fl oz/200ml)
   unsweetened coconut cream

¾ cup (6.7fl oz/200ml) cold water

4 ice cubes

1 tsp freshly grated ginger root

⅓ cup frozen blueberries

1 tsp vanilla extract

1. Combine the ingredients in a large blender.

2. Blend on high for 1 minute or until the mixture is smooth and creamy.
   Serve promptly.

Tip For an extra protein boost that will help keep you feeling full, add 1 tablespoon chia
seeds. (Nutrition with chia seeds: 418 calories, 39g total fat, 7.5g total carbs, 6.5g net
carbs, and 6g protein.)

NUTRITION PER SERVING	//	350 CALORIES	//	35g TOTAL FAT	//	10g TOTAL CARBS	//	8g NET CARBS	//	4g PROTEIN

GLUTEN FREE **SUGAR FREE**

Affogato

Affogato is an Italian dessert, which literally means
"drowned." Traditionally, affogato is made with vanilla
ice cream, a shot of espresso, and a shot of amaretto,
which is an Italian liqueur. This version removes the sugar!

PREP TIME: **10 MINUTES**   COOK TIME: **NONE**   PASSIVE TIME: **3 HOURS**

MAKES: 6 SERVINGS
SERVING SIZE: 1

2 cups Vanilla Ice Cream
  (see p. 148), divided
6fl oz (180ml) espresso, divided

For the "amaretto"
4 tsp water
1fl oz (30ml) vodka
1 tsp granular erythritol
¼ tsp vanilla extract
¼ tsp almond extract

1. Make the "amaretto" by combining the water, vodka, erythritol, vanilla extract, and almond extract in a sealable container. Stir until the erythritol is dissolved, then seal the container and transfer to the fridge for 3 hours.

2. Add ⅓ cup ice cream to each of 6 serving glasses. Pour 2 teaspoons of the amaretto over the ice cream in each glass, then pour 1 ounce of the espresso over the top of each serving. Serve promptly.

Tip If you don't have an espresso machine, combine 6 teaspoons instant espresso powder with 60 ounces (180ml) hot water to make the espresso.

| NUTRITION PER SERVING | 196 CALORIES | 17.5g TOTAL FAT | 3g TOTAL CARBS | 2.7g NET CARBS | 3g PROTEIN |

⊗ **NUT FREE** ⊛ **GLUTEN FREE** ⊛ **SUGAR FREE**

Vanilla Ice Cream

This recipe is much richer and less icy than virtually any
other keto ice cream recipe you'll try. The lecithin in the
egg yolks creates a smooth and creamy texture,
and also makes the ice cream more scoopable.

PREP TIME: **15 MINUTES**	COOK TIME: **30 MINUTES**	PASSIVE TIME: **1 HR 15 MINS**

MAKES: 6 SERVINGS
SERVING SIZE: ⅓ CUP
(approximately 2.8oz/80g)

4 large egg yolks
4 tbsp granulated erythritol
1 cup (7.7fl oz/230ml) heavy
   whipping cream
½ cup (4fl oz/120ml) water
1 vanilla bean, seeded

1. In a medium heatsafe glass bowl, combine the egg yolks and erythritol. Whisk until the ingredients are well combined and the mixture becomes creamy. Set aside.

2. In a medium saucepan placed over medium heat, combine the whipping cream, water, vanilla bean pod, and vanilla seeds. Heat until the mixture comes to a gentle simmer (make sure the mixture doesn't boil), then remove the pan from the heat and discard the vanilla bean pod.

3. Begin tempering the ingredients by very slowly adding the heated cream mixture to the egg yolk mixture while continuously whisking. (Be very careful not to add the cream too quickly; otherwise, the egg yolk mixture may curdle).

4. Once the ingredients are combined, transfer the entire mixture back to the saucepan and place over medium heat. Heat for 5–7 minutes, stirring continuously, until the mixture just begins to thicken. Remove the pan from the heat and set aside to cool for 10 minutes.

5. Transfer the cooled mixture to a large bowl and cover with plastic wrap, making sure the plastic wrap is resting on the surface of the mixture to prevent a skin from forming on the surface. Transfer to the fridge to chill for a minimum of 1 hour.

6. Pour the mixture into an ice cream maker and churn for approximately 30 minutes. Store in a sealed container in the freezer for up to 2 weeks. (Allow the ice cream to soften for 10 minutes at room temperature before serving.)

Tip If you don't have an ice cream maker, you can place the ice cream in the freezer and stir every 30 minutes to break up the ice crystals that form during freezing. Repeat 2–3 times or until the desired consistency is achieved.

NUTRITION PER SERVING	173 CALORIES	17.5g TOTAL FAT	2g TOTAL CARBS	1.6g NET CARBS	3g PROTEIN

⊛ **GLUTEN FREE** ⊛ **SUGAR FREE**

Ice Cream Cookie Sandwiches

These sandwiches combine my famous chocolate chip cookies with a delicious ice cream center for a perfect pairing! This recipe is sugar-free, low-carb, and undeniably delicious. Just be sure to make enough to share!

PREP TIME: **10 MINUTES**	COOK TIME: **10 MINUTES**	PASSIVE TIME: **1 HOUR**

MAKES: 6
SERVING SIZE: 1

½ cup (3.5oz/100g) unsalted butter, melted

1 cup (4.5oz/130g) granular erythritol

1 tsp vanilla extract

1 large egg

2 cups (6oz/170g) almond meal

½ tsp xanthan gum

½ tsp baking powder

¼ tsp salt

½ cup (3oz/90g) sugar-free chocolate chips

1½ cups (9.5oz/270g) Vanilla Ice Cream (see p. 148)

1. Preheat the oven to 355°F (180°C).

2. Combine the melted butter and erythritol in a medium bowl. Using a hand mixer, beat the ingredients on medium for 1 minute, then add the vanilla extract and egg, and mix on low for an additional 20 seconds.

3. Add the almond meal, xanthan gum, baking powder, and salt. Mix until well combined. Add the chocolate chips and gently fold into the mixture.

4. Remove the dough from the bowl (you should be able to pick it up with your hands). Break the dough into 12 equal-sized pieces. Roll the pieces into balls, place them on a large baking tray, and use a fork to flatten the balls. Bake for 10 minutes, then transfer the cookies to the fridge to cool for a minimum of 30 minutes.

5. While the cookies are cooling, remove the ice cream from the freezer and let it sit at room temperature for 15 minutes to soften slightly.

6. Place one cookie upside down on a flat surface and place ¼ cup of the ice cream on top of the cookie. Place a second cookie on top of the ice cream and gently press down until the ice cream just reaches the edges of the cookies. Use a butter knife to smooth the edges. Store in an airtight container in the freezer for up to 1 week.

Tip Chocolate chip cookies are the best choice for this recipe, but coconut cookies or snickerdoodles also are delicious options.

NUTRITION PER SERVING	416 CALORIES	40g TOTAL FAT	7g TOTAL CARBS	3.5g NET CARBS	9g PROTEIN

NUT FREE ⦸ GLUTEN FREE SUGAR FREE

Chocolate Ice Cream

This recipe features rich chocolate flavor, without a hint
of sugar and virtually no carbs. It has a smooth and
creamy texture, and the lecithin in the egg yolks
helps make the ice cream more scoopable.

PREP TIME: **5 MINUTES**   COOK TIME: **30 MINUTES**   PASSIVE TIME: **1 HR 10 MINS**

MAKES: 6 SERVINGS
SERVING SIZE: ⅓ CUP
(approximately 2.8oz/80g)

1 cup (7.7fl oz/230ml) heavy
  whipping cream
½ cup (4fl oz/120ml) water
1 tbsp unsweetened cocoa
  powder
4 large egg yolks
4 tbsp granulated erythritol

1. In a medium saucepan placed over medium heat, combine the whipping cream, water, and cocoa powder. Heat until the mixture just comes to a simmer, then remove from the pan from the heat. Set aside.

2. In a medium heatsafe bowl, combine the egg yolks and erythritol. Whisk until the ingredients are completely incorporated and the egg yolks become creamy. (If you're using an electric hand mixer, set it to low speed.)

3. Begin tempering the ingredients by very slowly adding the heated cream mixture to the egg yolk mixture while continuously whisking.

4. Once the ingredients are combined, transfer the entire mixture back to the saucepan and place over medium heat. Heat for 5–7 minutes, stirring continuously, until the mixture just begins to thicken. Remove the pan from the heat and set aside to cool for 10 minutes.

5. Transfer the cooled mixture to a large bowl and cover with plastic wrap, making sure the plastic wrap is resting on the surface of the mixture to prevent a skin from forming on the surface. Transfer to the fridge to chill for a minimum of 1 hour.

6. Pour the mixture into an ice cream maker and churn for approximately 30 minutes. Store in a sealed container in the freezer for up to 2 weeks. (Allow the ice cream to soften for 10 minutes at room temperature before serving.)

Tip If you don't have an ice cream maker, you can place the ice cream in the freezer and stir every 30 minutes to break up the ice crystals that form during freezing. Repeat 2–3 times or until the desired consistency is achieved.

NUTRITION PER SERVING	172 CALORIES	17.5g TOTAL FAT	7g TOTAL CARBS	1.5g NET CARBS	3g PROTEIN

DAIRY FREE ⊗ **NUT FREE** ⊛ **GLUTEN FREE** ⊛ **SUGAR FREE** ⊘ **EGG FREE**

Coconut Ice Cream

This luscious treat combines two types of coconut to create one fantastic dessert. This recipe is super easy to make and will make you fall in love with the rich, creamy taste of coconut-based ice cream.

PREP TIME: **5 MINUTES**	COOK TIME: **35 MINUTES**	PASSIVE TIME: **1 HOUR**

MAKES: 7 SERVINGS
SERVING SIZE: ⅓ CUP
(approximately 2.8oz/80g)

1¾ cups (13.5fl oz/400ml) canned, unsweetened, full-fat coconut milk, chilled

1¾ cups (13.5fl oz/400ml) unsweetened coconut cream, chilled

2 tsp vanilla extract

15 drops stevia extract

¼ tsp guar gum (use only if the coconut milk or coconut cream do not already contain guar gum)

1. In a large bowl, combine the coconut milk, coconut cream, vanilla extract, and stevia. Mix until the ingredients are well combined. (If the coconut milk or coconut cream do not already contain guar gum, add the guar gum at this stage.)

2. Transfer the mixture to an ice cream maker and churn for 30–45 minutes or until the mixture becomes thick and creamy.

3. For a soft-serve style ice cream, serve promptly. For a harder, more scoopable ice cream, freeze for a minimum of 1 hour. (If freezing, remove from the freezer 15 minutes prior to serving to allow the ice cream to soften slightly.) Store in a sealed container in the freezer for up to 2 weeks.

Tip If you don't have an ice cream maker, combine all the ingredients in a large bowl and use a hand mixer to beat the ingredients until stiff peaks form. Serve immediately, or cover and transfer to the freezer.

NUTRITION PER SERVING	422 CALORIES	38g TOTAL FAT	6.5g TOTAL CARBS	5g NET CARBS	15g PROTEIN

Ⓓ **DAIRY FREE** Ⓝ **NUT FREE** Ⓖ **GLUTEN FREE** Ⓢ **SUGAR FREE** Ⓔ **EGG FREE**

Lemon Sorbet

What could be more refreshing than a soft sorbet
on a hot summer day? This tasty treat has only
10 calories per serving and features the zest and juice of
fresh lemons, both of which are packed with vitamin C.

PREP TIME: **15 MINUTES**	COOK TIME: **30 MINUTES**	PASSIVE TIME: **1 HR 15 MINS**

MAKES: 6 SERVINGS
SERVING SIZE: ⅓ CUP
(approximately 3.5oz/100g)

1 cup (8.3fl oz/235ml) fresh lemon
 juice (about 6 large lemons)
1 tbsp freshly grated lemon zest
1 cup (5.6oz/160g) granular
 erythritol
1 cup (8.3fl oz/235ml) water

1. In a medium saucepan placed over medium heat, combine the lemon juice, lemon zest, erythritol, and water. Heat, stirring frequently, until the erythritol is completely dissolved.

2. Remove the pan from the heat and let the mixture cool for 10 minutes, then transfer to the fridge to chill for a minimum of 1 hour.

3. Transfer the chilled mixture to an ice cream maker and churn for 30 minutes or until the sorbet becomes thick and icy.

4. Serve immediately, or transfer to an airtight container and store in the freezer for up to 2 weeks. (Allow the frozen sorbet to soften at room temperature for 10 minutes before serving.)

Tip If you don't have an ice cream maker, transfer the mixture to a large bowl and place in the freezer. Stir every 30 minutes for 3 hours or until the desired texture is achieved.

NUTRITION PER SERVING	10 CALORIES	0g TOTAL FAT	3g TOTAL CARBS	2.5g NET CARBS	0g PROTEIN

Index

A

B

C

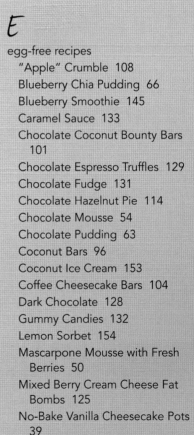